Haunted
North Carolina

Haunted
North Carolina

Ghosts and Strange Phenomena
of the Tar Heel State

Patty A. Wilson

Illustrations by Heather Adel Wiggins

STACKPOLE
BOOKS

Published by
STACKPOLE BOOKS
5067 Ritter Road
Mechanicsburg, PA 17055
www.stackpolebooks.com

Printed in the United States of America

10 9 8 7 6 5 4 3 2 1

FIRST EDITION

Cover design by Caroline Stover

Library of Congress Cataloging-in-Publication Data

Wilson, Patty A.
    Haunted North Carolina : ghosts and strange phenomena of the Tar Heel State / Patty A. Wilson ; illustrations by Heather Adel Wiggins. — 1st ed.
        p.   cm.
    Includes bibliographical references.
    ISBN-13: 978-0-8117-3585-8 (pbk.)
    ISBN-10: 0-8117-3585-0 (pbk.)
    1. Haunted places—North Carolina. 2. Ghosts—North Carolina. I. Title.
BF1472.U6W5575   2009
133.109756—dc22
                                            2009019333

Contents

Introduction

NORTH CAROLINA IS A STORIED LAND. THE AREA WAS WELL POPULATED before the first European arrival, with estimates of native populations running as high as forty thousand to fifty thousand people. The state has a history and culture that fades back into the mists of time.

The advent of European exploration brought change. The Italians and Spanish made brief forays into the area, but it was the British who chose to first settle there. Along with them came their culture and their diseases, forever changing the landscape of North Carolina.

The oldest European mystery in the Americas is that of Roanoke Island and what happened to the 110 settlers who came to the North Carolina coast to make a new life. The fate of the first English baby born in America, Virginia Dare, still remains a mystery to historians and archeologists.

Every successive wave of immigrants has had an impact on North Carolina. British occupations brought pirates, swashbuckling, and romance to the land. Settlers drove out the natives and scrambled to build their own stronghold in the New World. They tried to make a haven in which to raise their children, but disputes with the Indians brought war and blood.

From the Blue Ridge Mountains in the west to the region on the coast, this is a vast and varied state. North Carolina nurtured the very roots of this nation as one of the original colonies that fought for independence. It was also the setting for bloody conflict in the Civil War.

It should come as no surprise, then, that a state with this much history and passion is also a most haunted state. There are layers upon layers of ghost stories in every region, some dating back before European settlement. There are ghostly pirates and heroines, spirits in the Uwharrie Mountains, and phantoms on the islands along the Cape. In my research I have come to realize that a region's ghost stories represent the history of a people and reflect their culture, beliefs, and hopes. It is my pleasure to introduce you to these ghostly tales from grand old North Carolina, and I hope that you will gain a new appreciation for the Tar Heel State after reading them.

Coastal Region

ROMANCE AND MYSTERY SURROUND THE STRING OF ISLANDS OFF THE coast of North Carolina as well as the region on its eastern shore. The land is filled with enduring mysteries and tales of pirates and damsels in distress. The sea is the master here and many of the ghosts come from its very depths. Ghost ships ride the waves and beautiful, doomed women plunge themselves into the waters in an eternal bid to protect their honor and escape from even more unseemly fates. There is no end to the fascinating stories that come from this region. Devils and phantoms abound in the land where little Virginia Dare mysteriously disappeared and the Graveyard of Ships swallows sailors even today.

The Lost Colony

The first true mystery concerning Europeans in America is the odd disappearance of the Roanoke settlement. The fate of this little colony has captured the minds and hearts of people on both sides of the Atlantic Ocean and remains an enigma to this day.

The British of the sixteenth century were a people of conquest and colonization, but America posed a challenge. When the British arrived, they found many communities and nations of people already settled on the land. The European explorers believed they had rights to the land by virtue of the blood in their veins and the natives felt they had the rights by virtue of past possession. When two civilizations collide and both desire the same thing, however, it is inevitable that war and death will follow. But the natives were also people of compassion who had genuinely friendly personalities

On April 27, 1584, two British ships landed on Roanoke Island. The ships had been sent out by Sir Walter Raleigh with the blessing of Queen Elizabeth to explore the New World for possible colonization. Aboard were tradesmen, craftsmen, artists, and explorers, charged with the task of looking for exploitable resources, such as timber, gold, and fertile land.

The ships reached the Outer Banks on July 13, 1584, and the explorers sailed in small vessels to land. They put in at what is now Nags Head, North Carolina, and climbed hills or dunes to see what was before them. They quickly realized that they were on a barrier island and decided to move on to the northern end of Roanoke. There they found a palisaded village of natives who were quite hospitable to the English. When the men returned to England, they brought with them two natives, who were a curiosity for the British nobility.

Queen Elizabeth and her advisors were most happy with the descriptions, artist drawings, and the natives who were presented to her. She made Raleigh the Chief Lord of the new lands and charged him to set up colonies and make the land prosper for the British Empire.

In accordance, Raleigh planned a second expedition to Roanoke Island. This time he sent seven ships with 150 men and provisions to set up the first colony. The two natives again sailed with the ships so that they might return home. It was hoped that they would sway any hostile natives by telling them about how well they were treated. Some of the men from the first voyage also accompanied this new enterprise. Their help would be invaluable once they reached land again.

The second expedition reached Ocracoke Island on June 26, 1585, and began exploring with a view as to where they should set up the colony. They finally settled on Roanoke Island on July 27, and chose a spot where the river was wide enough to allow a ship to come inland.

The new governor, Ralph Lane, had a military background and immediately set about building a fort. He sent out expeditions to see what could be exploited and angered the local natives when he burned down an entire village over a misunderstanding about a silver cup. Lane's outright theft and aggression alienated the natives and led to warfare, which broke out by the summer of 1586.

Lane had requested more supplies shortly after beginning to build the fort on the east end of Roanoke Island, but the supply ships were delayed, leaving the natives as the only means of support. Of course at this point, they were not inclined to help the English. The one hundred and fifty men grew more desperate with each passing day. When Sir Francis Drake arrived with twenty-three ships and anchored in the harbor at Roanoke on June 9 of that year, many of the colonists and explorers begged him to take them home, which he subsequently did, making space for them onboard the ships.

Even Lane had to admit the colony had failed, and he himself boarded one of Drake's ships and returned to England. Fifteen days later, the supply ships did arrive. They brought along fifteen more men to join the colony but found the fort abandoned. It was decided that the fifteen men would remain to hold the land for Raleigh and England and new colonists would be sent over.

Raleigh still believed that the Americas should be colonized and gathered up another convoy of ships to sail to Roanoke Island in 1587. This group, led by Gov. John White, included women and children and was much less military in composition. Each planter who successfully settled in the new colony was to be given at least five hundred acres of land. This promise attracted 117 people to join White in the venture, including his son-in-law and daughter, Annanias and Eleanor White Dare. Upon arrival, the colonists searched for the fifteen men they were told would greet them, but they found no one. The houses were in ruins, the fort was partly destroyed, and the forestland had reclaimed the area, with vines and grasses growing on the structures. The colonists found the skeletal remains of one man who had been murdered and presumed that the natives had either killed the rest or taken them away.

The first order of business was to rebuild the fort and make shelters. It was too late in the year to plant crops, and Governor White realized that he must immediately send for more provisions. He feared that the provisions would be delayed unless he went in person to request them, but he delayed for a short time because his daughter was about to give birth. White's grandchild, Virginia, was born on August 18, 1587, and she would become notable in history as the first English child born in the Americas.

Only nine days after Virginia's birth, Governor White bid his family farewell and boarded the ship for England. Before he departed, he met with a council to develop some signals in the event of a problem to indicate what happened and where he should look if the colony had to move. In that case, White was to look for words carved in wood at the fort site. If the colonists had to leave under duress or were at war, they were to carve a cross above the words.

What happened at the colony after White left would forever remain a mystery. It was four years before he could return to Roanoke Island. Once he was in England, he was unable to persuade the queen or anyone else to give him ships for the provisions. England was at war with Spain and that took precedence over everything else. Sailors and other men were conscripted into service and ships could not be sacrificed for a journey to America. White languished in frustration and anger as he worried that the colony was suffering. At last, three years later, White was supplied with men and provisions, and on March 20, 1590, he sailed back to Roanoke.

On August 18, the men arrived on Roanoke's shore and saw smoke coming from the island. Surely it was a good sign, as White noted. But he soon understood, upon landing, that it meant nothing. The smoke appeared to be smoldering dead trees, probably blasted by lightning. They found the fort abandoned and the houses pulled down. A palisade made of thick tree trunks surrounded the fort. On one trunk was carved the word CROATOAN. Also the letters CRO were carved on a nearby tree. White was not alarmed at first. He knew that the Croatan Indians lived on a nearby island and had been friendly to the colonists, and the carvings were without the cross that signified danger. White wanted to explore the Croatoan Island (today called Hatteras Island) the following day, but a terrible storm erupted, keeping the men away. In need of supplies after their long voyage, the ship's captain insisted that they leave for the West Indies, despite White's protests. In great fear and sadness, he watched the islands drift away. He vowed to come back and search for his family, but that would never happen. A lack of funding would prohibit White from ever returning again to North Carolina.

In 1607, when Jamestown was established in Virginia, Capt. John Smith began inquiries among the local population on the whereabouts of the colonists from Roanoke. He was told that the colonists had split into two bands. Chief Powhatan, who despised the whites, bragged that some of the colonists had taken up residence with Chesapeake Indians, but that he had attacked the villages and slain them. He offered as proof a musket barrel, a brass mortar, and other European artifacts. But in 1612, the residents of Jamestown were told that some of the Roanoke colonists were still alive and living nearby. They began a search but never found any trace of them.

Since that time, many theories have been offered up to solve the mystery of what happened to the Roanoke colonists. There is some evidence to suggest that the Pembroke Indians took them in, and they assimilated and intermarried, which was common with that group and would explain the light hair and skin and blue eye color of some of the Pembrokes.

Whatever the truth is, the story of the Lost Colony has become an enduring part of North Carolina's history, and it is doubtful if the mystery will ever be solved. There are some who believe that the colonists who died still haunt the island.

Virginia Dare and the White Deer

There is a legend that explains the fate of little Virginia Dare, as well as the appearance of a ghostly white deer in Hatteras.

According to the legend, Chief Manteo of the Croatan tribe was returning from a fishing expedition when he learned that the British village on Roanoke was to be attacked by Chief Powhatan. Manteo slipped into the village to warn his friends. It was decided that the villagers would leave and a few brave men would stay behind to slow down the attack so that the others could escape to safety. Manteo knew of a secret tunnel through the caves that would bring the villagers out to canoes that he would have waiting there. He did rescue most of the villagers, including the beautiful, blond baby, Virginia Dare.

Manteo took the refugees to his own village at Hatteras, where he offered them asylum. The grateful villagers settled in and married within the tribe. There is biological evidence to suggest that at least part of this story is true, as some members of Manteo's tribe, like the Pembrokes, had fair skin, blond hair, and blue eyes. This could well be the legacy of the lost colonists.

According to the story, Virginia was much admired as she grew up, for her fair looks were exotic to the dark-haired people. She was a lovely young woman and many of the men wanted to wed her, but Virginia did not want to get married.

Among those who pushed the hardest for Virginia to choose a mate was the medicine man, Chico. He wanted to take Virginia as his wife and longed to make his bid for her. Virginia, though, did not love Chico and turned her eyes toward another young man whom she had grown up with, a tall, handsome chief named Wanchese, who was a fierce hunter and warrior.

Chico was furious that Virginia favored Wanchese and vowed to make her unacceptable to him and every other man. He heard of a very powerful potion that could shift the shape of a person into an animal and decided to use it on Virginia. He called upon the powers of the sea and upon the spirits of the island to transform the beautiful young girl.

When he was sure that his spell would work, he lured Virginia into the forest where he tricked her into drinking the mixture.

Virginia had known Chico all of her life and was not suspicious when he gave her the brew. She drank it and moments later fell ill. Chico chanted and called upon the spirits as Virginia writhed in pain. When at last Virginia rose again, she appeared to be a white doe. Terror and confusion filled the girl's heart. She leapt forward and bounded away on strong legs.

Virginia ran until she came to a stream to get a drink. When she saw her reflection in the water, she realized she could not go back to her village. She could not appear before her beloved Wanchese, for he was a great hunter and might slay her. She would have to hide in the forest.

For some months the hunters saw the white deer, but they could not kill it. The doe seemed to anticipate their every move. It was as if it was more spirit than real. Wanchese had been devastated by the disappearance of Virginia, and he wanted to find the spirit deer in hope that it could tell him where she had gone.

An old hunter told Wanchese that only silver-tipped arrows could bring down a spirit deer, and so Wanchese had made such arrows. One day, he stalked the deer and at last found it near a stream. The doe bowed her head to drink and Wanchese brought his bow up. For a second, the deer raised its head and Wanchese hesitated, but then he let the silver-tipped arrow fly.

As the arrow struck the doe, it let out a human scream. Wanchese suddenly realized that this was not a deer at all but rather a human bewitched in some way. He ran forward and fell before the doe. It looked up at him with quivering sides. From the beast's lips came a voice. "I am Virginia Dare" the deer gasped before it died.

Since that time and until this day, a white deer is occasionally seen on Hatteras, and those who know the tale believe that it is the spirit of young Virginia haunting the island.

The Ghost Ship Crissie Wright

It was a cold winter's night on January 11, 1886, and it was a terrible night to be a sailor plying the waters near North Carolina. On board the *Crissie Wright*, Capt. Jeb Collins struggled with a dilemma. The seas had turned hostile with a bitter storm. Wind buffeted the ship, forcing him to lower the sails. Ice froze in the rigging and made the deck dangerous to traverse. Wave upon wave washed across the frozen deck, adding to the layers of ice. The men were bundled up, but nothing could keep out the bitter cold of the frigid water for long. The ship faced the most dangerous part of its journey as it prepared to cross the Diamond Shoals headed toward Cape Lookout. In such a rough sea, it could well be a suicide mission.

Captain Collins was a seasoned sailor who knew the area well. At last, he decided to turn back from the shoals and weather the storm in the deep water where the risks were fewer. In a gruff voice, he called his orders and the men hurried to obey. The men slipped and slid along the deck, but soon the ship was anchored both at the fore and aft sides to ride the storm out before crossing the shoals. On Shackleford Banks, the little town of Diamond City watched the hapless ship. The people began preparations for a dis-

aster. The men built a large bonfire on the beach as a beacon, and hot coffee was brewed and broth made to feed any survivors. The men attempted to launch the heavy whaling ships, but they had no luck; the sea would not let them set sail that night. One ship they tried to launch capsized in the waves and several men were hurt. Finally, the would-be rescuers took shelter and waited.

On board the *Crissie Wright*, the men were helpless as the battering waves rose and crashed down again and again upon the deck. Even the most hardened sailors among them were silent as the storm raged on. The men had done all they could do and now they were able only to wait out the storm to its end.

On deck, Captain Collins kept a sharp watch. Everyone's fingers and toes were numb and the spray had frozen across the men's faces, leaving white eyebrows and beards. Suddenly, a wave rose up and crashed on the deck, sending the ship dipping downward. There was a terrible crack and the mainmast broke. Rigging dangled as the waves hungrily licked at the broken mast. The ship took another terrible dip, and a wave sent the broken mast ahead like a bludgeon, punching a hole into the decking. Water immediately began pouring through on the men below. There were screams and shouts as the men hurried to fix the hole before the ship was swamped.

Another wave crashed in from above and the ship shuddered, ripping the planking. Men fought to get topside to help lower the lifeboats, but the waves plucked at them. Two men were nearly swept overboard. It was impossible to launch the lifeboats in such weather.

Another wave struck the ship and swallowed Captain Collins and two mates. The men now screamed for mercy, but it did no good. The *Crissie Wright* lost the fight. The ship foundered and filled with water. Men tried to hold on with numbed fingers. On the shore, the townspeople waited as the night grew even more bitterly cold. They huddled by fires to keep warm and thought silently of the men that were struggling aboard the vessel just off their coast. It was daylight before they could launch a rescue attempt. At first light, a sturdy whaling boat hurried toward the wreckage of the *Crissie Wright*. What the men found was horrible. Of the seven sailors, only four were left aboard. They had wrapped themselves in the mainsail canvas to wait out the storm, but three of them had frozen to death. Only the cook, a large beefy man, had survived. The rescuers took him ashore where he was given medical treatment, but he was never well again, physically or mentally.

Ever since that bitter winter, there have been those who live along the shore who say that on wild, stormy nights, the ghost of the *Crissie Wright* once again rides the waves. Her crew fights their futile struggle for survival once more and the sounds of the poor, doomed ship can be heard.

Captain Harper's Encounter

In the mid-1800s, Capt. John Harper was owner and master of a steamer named the *Wilmington*, which made a daily trip from Wilmington to Southport by way of Lower Cape Fear. On occasion, he also ran special chartered trips. Captain Harper and his vessel became well known among the traveling public, largely because of his wonderful ability as a storyteller. He regaled his passengers with tales of the area and of his own adventures.

One strange tale Captain Harper often told was called the "Colonial Apparition." He prefaced the story by saying that the night of the events was one of the most frightening of his life. It begins on a stormy, cold winter's night, when the captain was in the wheelhouse watching closely over the ship's course. Despite the terrible weather, Captain Harper was not overly concerned and attempted the crossing. But when he looked out of the little glass pilothouse, he shuddered. The wind whipped around the vessel, battering it dangerously. Waves rose up, threatening to swamp her, and a cold drizzle covered most of the deck with ice. The wild winds pushed the steamer around, and Peter Jorgensen, one of the deckhands, was taking constant depth soundings. Captain Harper remained calm, as if he knew that by instinct alone he could pilot the ship safely to port. Also aboard that night were his crew and one passenger who had come to join Captain Harper in the wheelhouse of the ship. The passenger's name was MacMillan, and he watched the weather raging around the ship.

"You know," MacMillan said, "I have an ancestor who nearly was executed in this very area during the Revolution. Have you ever heard the story of the Scottish Highlanders who were executed at Brunswick?"

The captain replied that he had not heard this tale and bid MacMillan to continue. "Well my great-grandfather, William MacMillan, was a talented Scottish soldier, and he was invited by none less than Governor Johnston to come and take up the cause. Great-grandfather did come along with a group of fellow soldiers. They fought for the American cause and made homes in North Carolina.

"Now it was near the end of the American Revolution when events transpired that led to the executions. In September of 1781, Colonel Fanning, a leader among the Tories, set his sights upon this area." MacMillan waved his hand toward the window.

"Fanning was famous for being able to obtain valuable information from prisoners. He did this by targeting people with a good deal of probable knowledge and then capturing them. He'd apply various tortures to the captives until they talked. His methods were crude but most effective, and everyone in the Brunswick area was worried lest they come to the attention of Colonel Fanning.

"Fanning began taking prisoners by setting up a surprise attack on Hillsboro. He managed to capture the governor and other leading people. He gathered the prisoners together and marched them toward Wilmington, where he planned to turn them over to the British along with whatever information he could glean. Along the way, Fanning took prisoner anyone he felt might be useful. Among those he captured were my great-grandfather and two other Scottish Highlanders.

"Fanning learned that Scottish Highlanders had been forced to take an oath to the king of England, which they had renounced once they had come to settle in the Cape Fear area along with a good number of other Scottish folks. Now Fanning decided to make an example of the Scottish traitors. He would try them and execute them.

"The men were interred in an old slave ship in the bay at Brunswick. It was a filthy, vile place for the poor men, and they attempted to escape but to no avail. A mockery of a trial was set up and the three Scottish men were found guilty. The first two were brought out in irons and executed. Then they led my great-grandfather to the tree where he would be killed. For only a moment they loosened his bonds so that they could wrap the chains around the execution tree. In that second Grandfather lunged forward and

made a mad dash for freedom. Grandfather hid in the brush and moved quickly and quietly along. He never stopped and never rested until he reached his own cabin door. In approximately twenty-four hours he traveled no less than seventy miles.

"Grandfather was never rearrested and he lived to a ripe old age, but he never forgot those events, and he never forgot those men who died there that day. He often told the story and you could see by his eyes that his surviving haunted him in some way." MacMillan turned his eyes to the storm-tossed night raging around the snug little wheelhouse and sighed.

Captain Harper followed his passenger's gaze. He knew that they were just passing the Brunswick area. Then he scanned the waters for signs of the shoreline.

MacMillan cleared his throat and began to talk softly again. "You know that the local slaves used to say that on stormy nights the spirits of the two executed men would rise and walk. Have you ever heard any such tales, captain?" MacMillan inquired.

Captain Harper nodded. "Aye, I've heard such tales, but they're barely whispered these days. The tales were told to me long ago and without the rich knowledge that your family history has brought to the story."

"If spirits are loosed in that area," MacMillan maintained, "then they must be those of the executed men that Grandfather told me about. Surely they'd have every reason to not lie peacefully in their graves. In fact, I've looked into the ghostly tale and learned that on more than one occasion the spirits have also been seen in a boat upon the waters, rowing toward ships. I believe that they are looking for passage back home to Scotland, but that I can't prove."

Despite Captain Harper's intense interest, he found himself quickly shifting his focus as the ship ran into difficulties. The vessel was tossed and the captain and crew struggled to keep it upright in the waters. Through long hours, fear grew in Captain Harper's normally placid heart.

Peter Jorgensen brought the captain more bad news. The ship had lost its course and they were unable to find their location with the instruments. Within moments, the ship's keel slid over the jetties and the craft was caught. There was nothing that could be done until first light. The captain found the ship to be basically sound, however, and decided to weather the storm stuck on the jetties. The crewmen retired to the furnace room, where they could dry off and lose the terrible chill that enveloped them that night, but Jorgensen remained on watch. The poor mate was buffeted by the winds and icy rain, yet he kept walking the deck and looking out anxiously into the darkness.

Midnight came and Captain Harper was awake and terribly frightened that he had made a bad decision by sailing that night. Jorgensen, unaware of the time, struggled to stay upright and warm against the biting winter wind. Vigilant as always, he swung his lantern and kept walking the decks. Suddenly, in the leading edge of the light, he thought he saw something. He stopped and held the lantern high; then he stepped closer and froze again. He saw a man, dripping wet, standing there holding the railing, as if he had just climbed out of the water. The man turned toward Jorgensen, who nearly cried out. Ice was frozen in the man's beard and hair. A look of gaunt horror etched his face. Fearing the specter would bring harm to the crew, Jorgensen lunged forward to knock this watery spirit back into the depths, but his hands plunged through it. There was no substance.

Jorgensen fled to the wheelhouse. Inside he found Captain Harper and MacMillan talking. The two men listened in shock as poor Jorgensen poured out his ghostly tale. Had the captain not known Jorgensen so well, he would have accused the man of imbibing alcohol, but one look at Jorgensen's face and shaking hands was enough to assure the captain that the man spoke the truth. Quickly Captain Harper and MacMillan donned rain slickers and made their way to the point on deck where Jorgensen had seen the apparition. They saw nothing.

The two men returned to the relative warmth and comfort of the wheelhouse and were only beginning to warm themselves when a seagull crashed through the wheelhouse windows, bringing in the raging storm. The bleeding, quivering bird skidded to a stop at MacMillan's feet and died. MacMillan became rather unnerved and insisted that the bird was an ill omen. There was yet more trouble to befall the vessel, he declared.

Captain Harper tried to remain calm. He felt a surge of relief when the vessel shifted with the rising tide and began to float again.

To calm Jorgensen and MacMillan, the captain began joking. Fear clutched his own heart, however, but he refused to give vent to it.

He ordered Jorgensen back to watch, joking about keeping a weather eye out for more ghosts. Jorgensen failed to find the comment funny, but he returned to duty. MacMillan calmed, as the captain steered the ship along.

Suddenly, a terrible scream rang out. The crew came tumbling out on deck, where Jorgensen insisted that he had heard a siren shrieking. No one else saw or heard a thing. Captain Harper ordered the vessel to stop until he was sure that all were safe. In an instant, the ship gave a sickening roll and lurched sideways. The vicious winds buffeted it, and the captain realized the ship was in a trough. He ordered the men on deck to start watches around the ship. As they tumbled out in their warmest garb, another terrible scream filled the air. The men muttered darkly as the painful scream died down. They peered into the darkness against the lashing rain and the howling wind. Without the sound of the engines, the storm seemed to growl in fury.

Suddenly, a vessel appeared in the distance. The men all thought that they had to be imagining things. The ship bobbing toward them through the storm was an ancient slave ship. Then another terrible scream filled the night air. It sounded as if someone was being tortured aboard the foul vessel. The captain, vaguely aware of MacMillan's presence at his shoulder, watched in horror. When he turned to look at the shore, he realized that they were in approximately the same location as MacMillan had described in his tale.

The slave ship loomed closer and now a frightful change took place. The vessel began to glow with a soft green light that illuminated it, so that the men could see it more clearly. Seaweed clung to the vessel and the terrible screams came again and again, squeezing the hearts of those who heard them each time they tore the air.

The captain ordered that the ancient vessel be secured, and his men tossed out a line. In the dim glow of the ship, they could see two men bound and shackled. They appeared to be mere skeletons with skin stretched over them. The two then cried out in pain at their bonds and raised futile arms to catch the towline.

Jorgensen pulled in the towline and re-coiled it for another throw. The men were silent in fear as they watched and waited. The captain ordered that the line be thrown again and Jorgensen obliged. Just as Jorgensen let the rope loose, a gray wave smashed into the hulk and seemed to swallow the line up.

The men aboard the *Wilmington* waited in horror but the slave ship did not resurface. For several moments they all scanned the darkness, but the slave ship was gone.

Quickly Captain Harper ordered the engines restarted and he set up a new watch. Then he ordered his men back to work. Returning to the wheelhouse, he began to settle down and think about what he had seen and heard that night. Then a watchman burst in. "Captain, we've spotted a wreck," he announced and waited for further orders.

Captain Harper turned to look and ordered the ship to swerve to avoid the wreck. The vessel was floating upside down on the waters and two men clung to its slippery bottom. The men were half frozen and could barely cry out for help. The captain ordered his men to rescue the poor survivors, and within minutes they were brought aboard the *Wilmington*, shivering and thanking their rescuers. Jorgensen cried out when he saw the face of the bearded man, for it was the same face he had seen at the ship's railing earlier that night, although that seemed impossible.

The survivors were taken inside and given food and dry clothing. When they were settled, they told the group that they were the last two survivors of the shipwreck. Five other men had died when the vessel capsized in the waves. The two men had clung to the hull of their ship and cried out for help hour after hour in the hope that someone would hear their cries.

Though Captain Harper surely had his own ideas of why the events of that fateful night had played out the way they did, he never spoke of it. Did the ghosts of the two doomed men from the slave ship appear and guide the *Wilmington* to rescue the survivors of the shipwreck? Well, what the captain thought he never revealed aloud. He only told the tale and allowed the listeners to come to their own conclusions.

The Spirits of Fort Fisher

In war there are many ways to win. You can outthink, outmaneuver, or overwhelm the enemy. You also can disrupt the supply lines, because without food and ammunition, an army will soon stop functioning. That was what happened at Fort Fisher. It became the last stronghold protecting the Confederate supply lines for the Army of Northern Virginia and its strategic importance cannot be overstated. In May 1861, Maj. Charles Bolles and his men began work on artillery batteries in the area that would later be called Fort Fisher. Bolles and two other officers believed that at some point Fort Fisher might become strategically significant.

By July 1862, Col. William Lamb was given command of a few sand batteries with a mounting of approximately twenty-three guns at Fort Fisher. Colonel Lamb realized the fort was the key to protecting both the Cape Fear area and the city of Wilmington, which was a major supply port, so he began building it up. The fort was constructed mostly of earth and sand, which made it far superior to brickwork forts when shelled, because the materials absorb the shock of the explosions. By the end of the Civil War, Fort Fisher covered approximately one-third of a mile of land and more than a mile of sea defense. The fort was built by an estimated five hundred men, mostly slaves and free blacks. When it was completed, twenty-two guns were mounted on a line of twelve-foot-high batteries facing the ocean. At the south side, two batteries, sixty feet high and forty-five feet high respectively, were also built. Large earthen mounds were used to house a hospital, telegraph office, and other needed facilities. The land side was secured with twenty-five guns on fifteen mounds. The mounds were more than thirty-two feet high, and the inside rooms were used for the storage of munitions. Tunnels were dug between the mounds so that snipers would be unable to take advantage of troop movements. A nine-foot-tall palisade fortified the land side for the entire length of the fort.

Lamb's foresight would prove vital to the Confederate Army. By 1864, Fort Fisher was the Confederacy's largest fort and was charged with protecting the last major supply area in Wilmington. It was now under the command of Gen. William H. C. Whiting, brother-in-law of Major Bolles, who originally built the first structures on the ground. Colonel Lamb, however, remained on duty there. Under the protection of Fort Fisher, Confederate naval travel continued and allowed British ships, called blockade runners, to smuggle supplies from Canada, Bermuda, and the Bahamas past the Federal blockades. Union warships were forced to stay far from the shoreline by Fort Fisher's deadly guns.

On December 24, 1864, Union forces launched an all-out attack on Fort Fisher. The fort held, and after two days of stalemate fighting, the Federals retreated. It seemed as if Fort Fisher was impregnable. For nearly two weeks, the Union forces looked for weak links in the fort but found none. They knew, however, that they needed to take Fort Fisher in order to break the supply lines and win the Civil War.

On January 12, 1865, a second attack on the fort was mounted. U.S. warships set up a steady barrage of shelling on the ocean side for two and a half days. At last, on the third day, the Union army broke its way in the fort where hand-to-hand combat ensued. By nightfall, the fort surrendered. Colonel Lamb and General Whiting had both been mortally wounded before the fort fell. Within a few weeks, Wilmington fell to the Union forces and the supply lines of the South were broken. The war would soon be over.

More than two thousand men died in the attacks at the fort. General Whiting himself succumbed to his injuries and died at a prison camp in New York, but it is believed that he haunts Fort Fisher, because he never overcame the loss of the fort.

Today, less than ten percent of the fort remains. Although most of it was reclaimed by time and the ocean, it has become a national historic landmark. The palisade has been reconstructed and a visitor's center offers films and displays about the fort and its importance to the Civil War.

The first known reported sighting of General Whiting occurred only a few years after the end of the Civil War. According to local lore, a group of Confederate veterans who had been stationed at Fort Fisher returned there to walk through the area and remember their fallen friends and brothers. They continued their reunion far beyond the time they had planned. As they watched the sun sink low, one of them saw a motion on the parapets on the land side. In the last light, it appeared to him that it was an officer standing there. The man pointed out the figure to his comrades, but it was not necessary. Each man was already watching avidly. The unknown officer stood, looking landward as if watching for something. And then, in the sinking light, the shadows shifted and the man became harder to make out. He became indistinct, and then he was gone.

One of the old veterans turned and addressed the others. "That's about where he was the day he was shot, wasn't it?" Another concurred. No one said the words, but each man remembered a beloved officer named William Whiting whom they in private had affectionately called "Little Billy."

Through the years, other veterans who had served there caught a glimpse of General Whiting still watching. They all knew him and none of them doubted who he was. "You don't forget an officer who commands you in battle," they said when anyone scoffed at them.

For many years, other stories have circulated about footsteps that can be heard, as if unseen men are walking and working at the fort. Others say that General Whiting is still standing at the palisades, watching out and giving orders as if still trying to win the battle.

A new chapter was added to the haunting in the 1950s, when an old hermit named Robert Edward Harrell escaped from an elder care facility and took up residence at Fort Fisher in an old World War II bunker. Harrell could no longer stand elder care and decided to make his own way. He mostly lived off the land, raising a garden, fishing, and scavenging for food, but he also relied on the kindness of local folks to feed him occasionally. He earned a small amount of money, which he kept hidden in jars and cans he had stashed around the area. He spent most of his time outside and often slept out in the fresh air.

Old Harrell lived at Fort Fisher for seventeen years. During that time, many folks befriended the old man, and they respected him for his self-reliant attitude. He became a bit of a local celebrity. Reporters wrote articles about him and at least one documentary was shot in which he was extensively interviewed. On occasion, local ruffians gave the old man trouble, but no one thought that it would ever get out of hand.

On June 4, 1972, local police were notified that Harrell's dead body had been found in his bunker. It was a strange sight though, and the story would only get stranger as time went on. The police chief and the local crime scene photographer went to the site and had to remove the boards that Harrell had presumably placed up against the entrance to the bunker to get inside. Harrell lay on the ground, arms and legs spread out and his raincoat bunched up around his neck. There were footprints around the body in the sand. Outside, the men found what looked like drag marks running thirty feet from the bunker and also the treadmarks of a four-wheel-drive vehicle. The photographer insisted that it looked like Harrell had been dragged into the bunker by his feet and the boards were then placed up to shield the body from discovery. But the police chief concluded that Harrell had suffered a heart attack outside, where he usually slept, and then crawled inside and placed the boards up before succumbing to death.

It was a strange tale and not many local folks believed the police chief's version of the hermit's death. The local coroner only added to the controversy when he stated that Harrell had died of natural causes without doing an autopsy.

Within six months, the case was closed because of lack of evidence. When it was reopened and Harrell's body was exhumed, it was badly decomposed and little could be learned from it. Many people who lived in the area and knew Harrell believe that the old man met with foul play. They speculate that he was killed by local ruffians who abused the man too much that night and then tried to cover it up. Others think he was killed for his hidden money.

Whatever the reason for Harrell's death, many locals say that on certain nights his voice can be heard arguing with someone as he relives his last moments on earth. The voices then fade away toward the bunker and stop. Is Harrell trying to name his killer or is he simply haunting the place where he had lived wild and free?

The Cursed Town of Bath

Bath is the oldest town in North Carolina. Back in 1747, the little seaport was a bustling place, catering to the seafaring trade. Rowdy sailors and pirates could be found making merry in the public houses, where fallen women danced and liquor flowed freely. It seemed to Rev. George Whitefield that Bath was a town in need of salvation.

Reverend Whitefield was a well-known traveling evangelist, part of a vast movement of religious fervor at the time called the Great Awakening. He held open-air meetings, preached in chapels and churches in villages and ports, and even in backyards and homes. He was a man who dedicated his life to his faith and spreading his Christian beliefs to others.

The evangelist was a strange, stiff-necked fellow, however. He traveled in a wagon in which he carried his own coffin. He had his death planned as well as his salvation. When he died, he said, he wanted his coffin ready for him. Stranger still, Whitefield slept in his coffin at night. He said that he preferred it to sleeping in the dens of sin that served the public with lodging.

Whitefield was not afraid to preach against any sin, and he believed there were plenty of sins in Bath—gambling, drinking, cursing, loud music, and dancing. Of all the deadly sins Whitefield preached against, he hated dancing the most.

At his revivals, Whitfield poured out his wrath on the sinners of this little port town. The men and women who made their money on these sinners, however, did not appreciate hearing about their damnation. They turned a blind eye to the more unsavory establishments, not wanting to lose their own income.

Whitefield spent weeks in Bath trying to muster up a decent congregation. A few people supported him, but on the whole, Bath was not a town in search of salvation. It seemed that the sinners had control and they liked it that way.

Despite Whitefield's scathing sermons and his most diligent ministrations, the town of Bath resisted. Whitefield was infuriated by the unrepentant town. He finally decided to leave the den of sinners behind. He drove his wagon to the edge of town, climbed down, and took off his shoes. Like Jonah when he left Nineveh, Whitefield shook the dust of Bath from his shoes and cursed the little town. "I say to the village of Bath, village you shall remain, now and forever, forgotten by men and nations until such time as it pleases God to turn the light of his countenance again upon you."

Apparently the people of Bath should have put some credence in the strange minister's words, for the town has been plagued no less than three times by devastating fires, and it never grew into the world-class port it should have become. For some reason, the sailors and pirates moved on, and Bath is all but forgotten. It is now remembered only as the town that Whitefield cursed.

The Ghostly Prints at the Cutlar Farm

October 13, 1813, was a cool, pleasant Sunday on the Cutlar farm outside the city of Bath. Ed Cutlar and his family were hosting a community picnic and horse race. Women bustled about setting tables with multitudes of bowls and dishes, heaped with food. Children laughed and played. The men were playing horseshoes in the shade of the trees at the edge of the big field, or lounging around enjoying the last of the summer's warmth. Others gathered as they waited for the race, and the conversation naturally turned toward horse racing. One young man in the company was particularly boastful that day. Jesse Elliot believed himself to be the best rider in all of the area around Bath and was brash enough to say so.

Jesse may actually have been able to live up to his boast. He rode a sleek stallion named Fury and rarely ever lost a race. "No one can beat me," he boasted on that October afternoon. "There's no one in the whole area who can beat Fury and me in a horse race." Jesse dared anyone to challenge him that very day. No one took him up on the boast, but several people walked away in disgust over his arrogance.

Folks whispered their wishes that someone would beat Jesse Elliot and knock him down to size. Meanwhile, the races continued through the afternoon. When the gossip reached the ears of a young fellow from a neighboring town, he said he would challenge Jesse Elliot to a race and beat him. The challenge was issued and Jesse accepted. Money changed hands as betting began. Three other men entered the race. When the time for the race came, Jesse seemed unusually quiet and subdued. The young man from out of town baited him. "Don't ya think you're gonna win?" he chortled. Jesse remained quiet, but his face had the mottled look of an angry man.

Folks gathered around and the horses were taken to the starting spot. The master of ceremonies called attention. "Line up, boys," he shouted. A buzz went through the crowd before silence fell upon them.

Jesse looked around and bent over Fury's neck. He had the determined look of a madman. The master of ceremonies held his hand up, then brought it down decisively. "Go!" he shouted.

In that last second, Jesse dug his heels into Fury's flanks and screamed, "Make us win or take me to hell, Fury!"

With his shocking words still ringing in the ears of the spectators, Jesse shot forward as Fury bolted ahead of the pack. For just a moment the horse appeared to have already won the race, but then suddenly it came to a jarring stop in the middle of the track. Jesse was carried over the horse's head and flew forward. His head struck an old pine tree with a sickening thud and a horrified hush fell over the group for a few seconds. Suddenly, some of the men broke away from the crowd and ran toward Jesse's still body. One side of his head was crushed. When they rolled him over, there was no mistaking the blank look of death in the eye that survived the impact. After Jesse's death, the people of Bath no longer had a taste for horse races or Sunday picnics at the Cutlar farm. As time went on, folks began to notice some strange things about the old field where Jesse's last race was run. The beaten-down path of the track never faded away. No weeds or hay reclaimed the land. Nothing would grow there. The tree Jesse struck became strangely blighted on the side he had hit. It died on that side, but the piney branches hung in bountiful defiance on the other side of the tree for years.

No one wanted to use the field anymore, and eventually the Cutlars turned pigs out in the field. Even the hogs, reportedly, did not like the field. They avoided the track path and would not even cross it to get ears of corn. Eventually, the old pine tree was cut down and the community moved on. Some older people noticed that after the pine tree was cut down, four hoofprints appeared in the dirt around the stump. Folks whispered that the prints were from Fury. Others think that it's proof that Fury had stopped that fateful day because the Devil had come to collect Jesse's soul after Jesse made his unfortunate statement about winning or going to hell.

It is said that nothing can linger on the hoofprints. Not leaves nor grass nor trash can cover them for long. The prints are said to still exist today, but because the property is privately owned, no one can trespass to verify it. The owners are tired of the old tale and they do prosecute trespassers.

Does Jesse haunt the sight? Or, has the Devil marked it as his own? No one is sure, but those who remember the old stories have long asserted that something strange and sinister caused Fury to stop and throw his master that day.

Hatteras Jack

Early sailors were rough men who thrived on difficulty. They knew that sailing was dangerous business, as they fought the sea on a daily basis. Certain places were feared or respected because they were dangerous. Hatteras Inlet earned a reputation for being such a deadly stretch of water. It was filled with dangerous, shifting sand-bars and underwater hazards, but it was also a popular trade route that could not be avoided. The area near Bodie Island (originally Body's Island) was particularly difficult. Many ships were unsuccessful at negotiating the shifting sandbars and wrecked. According to legend, many bodies washed up on the shore and that is how the island got its name.

In the 1780s, sailors began to notice a white bottlenose dolphin that seemed to streak to the surface just before a ship entered Hatteras Inlet. Before long, some enterprising sailor realized that by following the dolphin he might avoid the sandbars. It seemed that the dolphin understood that, too. He streaked to the surface and called out if the the sailors lost sight of him in the waters. It seemed almost as if the dolphin had planned to help the ships—but could an animal do that on purpose?

Word spread about the amazing dolphin, affectionately called Hatteras Jack. Ship captains paused at the mouth of the inlet to see if the dolphin would appear. If Jack was absent, they blew their fog signal or rang a bell to call him in. It seemed to work. Hatteras Jack would come slicing through the water and call out to the vessel. Then slowly, Jack began his journey through the dangerous inlet. If the ship lagged behind, he paused and waited. When each ship reached the safety of the far side, Jack celebrated by jumping, frolicking, and leaping from the water. He made a great deal of noise, rolled around, and did the tail walk. Through the 1790s, Hatteras Jack was a celebrated hero, and in nearly any American port stories of his life-saving stunts were told. Then navigation techniques began to improve and Jack found that his efforts were no longer needed. One day, Jack failed to show up when a ship rang its bell. The vessel was forced to brave the inlet alone, and it was successful. For a long time, captains refused to believe that Jack was gone. They blew their whistles, but Jack would not appear.

No one knows what happened to Hatteras Jack. The sailing community assumed that he died. But some captains continued to see him. Even today, there are a few sailors who claim that a white bottlenose dolphin has appeared to them to guide them through the inlet during bad weather. Some say that this dolphin is none other than the ghost of Hatteras Jack.

The Mystery of the Carroll A. Deering

The morning of January 30, 1921, was cold and damp around the Cape Fear area. As people started their day, someone made a grisly discovery. Word spread quickly that a ship had run aground at Diamond Shoals. There was something strange about the ship though, and people speculated about the vessel as they made their way out to the shore. The ship was slowly sinking. This was odd, because the night before the weather had been fine, and now the ship's sails were still set wide, as if the breeze could push the schooner safely past the shoals. People noticed the name on this strange ship was *Carroll A. Deering*.

A group of men gathered at the ship and called out to those who should have been on board. Though they repeated their calls, there was no reply. Nothing stirred aboard the ship and at last it was decided that the Coast Guard must be called in. The Hatteras Inlet Coast Guard Station was notified and they quickly responded.

The Coast Guard contacted G. G. Deering Company, which owned the ship, and were authorized to board it. It had been nearly four days since the ship ran aground, and during that time the ship had sustained damage. When it seemed safe, the coastguardsmen climbed the sides of the ship and swung over the railing. They called out on the deck, but again there was no response. As the men moved around, they found no signs of distress. In the sleeping quarters, nothing was disturbed. No sick or dead men were found. There were no indications of a struggle. All was neat and clean.

In the galley, the men found a meal set on the table. The food was cold and there was no way to know exactly when it had been cooked, but there was little doubt that it had been recently laid on the boards.

There were no answers to be found in the captain's berth either. The logbook was missing, along with some of the navigational equipment. The men then checked the hold, but there was no cargo. They looked for the lifeboat and found it was missing. Even the anchors that held the lifeboat in place were gone. They did find a strange, long slice near the ladder on the side of the ship, but they had no idea what caused it. By the time the men had explored the entire vessel, they found that the only living creatures aboard the ship were two cats and some mice. It was all a complete mystery.

The Coast Guard issued an alert and every able-bodied person began a search. There were a multitude of inlets and little bays to explore, but despite the searchers' best efforts, not a single sign of the men or the lifeboat was ever found.

Inquiries were made and the names of the crew were identified. Their families were notified but none knew anything of the whereabouts of their lost loved ones. The investigation turned up other bits of information, but none of it made any sense. The usual captain of the vessel, F. Merritt, had taken leave of the ship due to illness shortly after the voyage had begun. The owners assigned Capt. W. M. Wormell to take command of the ship. A friend of Captain Wormell's later testified that the captain had confided to him that he disliked the first mate and the crew of eight men. They all got drunk in one previous instance and gave him trouble, and the captain anticipated a difficult voyage.

The passage of the vessel along its route was traced and nothing out of the ordinary was found. It had reported all as well at the lighthouses and check spots it passed. An officer of the Cape Lookout lightship, however, offered some strange observations. He claimed that when the *Carroll A. Deering* sailed by, a member of the crew called out with a megaphone, warning that all other ships should keep away, because they lost their anchor in a storm. There had been no storms, though, so how was that possible? He also reported that he saw people on the deck of the ship, but they seemed to be milling about and not working.

The Coast Guard later discovered that the schooner had just returned from Rio de Janeiro without picking up any cargo for the return trip. They also learned that a mysterious passenger boarded the ship in Rio. Who the person was could never be ascertained, and the purpose for the voyage also seemed shrouded in mystery. Furthermore, the ship was licensed to carry only ten men, and it seemed unlikely that Captain Wormell would violate the law. Answers to the mystery continued to elude the investigators.

The ship was eventually salvaged and the Coast Guard blew up what was left of it, so that it did not become a hazard on the shoals. Life moved on, and the name of the *Carroll A. Deering* was added to the list of vessels that had gone down in the area known as the

Graveyard of Ships. Within months of its loss, eight other vessels completely vanished in the area.

On cold winter nights, people recall the mystery of the *Carroll A. Deering*. Some say that during winter storms, you can hear the voices of the doomed crew crying out, trying to tell the story of their untimely demise. Others have claimed to have seen the *Carroll A. Deering*, or rather her wraith, sailing along Cape Fear. The ship is most often spotted on cold, clear winter nights. Whatever happened aboard the *Carroll A. Deering* seems to have left an imprint that has caused the ship to remain restless as it sails along, carrying a tragic secret.

Nell Cropsey

After the Civil War, the South was decimated. Carpetbaggers arrived, taking advantage of people who had property but no money. For many years, the price of land in the South was much cheaper than in the North, because many Southern families had to sell their acreage off in order to survive. Even at the end of the century, the situation was still desperate for some families. When the Cropsey family moved south, it was to purchase farmland. Mr. Cropsey had been a successful businessman in the North, but by 1898, he decided to turn his resources to farming. The Cropsey family settled in a lovely house, known locally as Seven Pines, along the Pasquotank River in Elizabeth City.

Cropsey's daughter, Nell, was seventeen years old when the family settled at Seven Pines. She had several handsome brothers and beautiful sisters, but she was said to be the prize of the lot. She was petite with a tiny waist and bouncing light brown curls. Her pale blue eyes danced with the lively excitement of youth. Nell could have any man she set eyes on, but the fellow who captured her interest was a young man named Jim Wilcox.

Jim was twenty-one when the couple first met, and he had fine prospects. He came from a good family and was well-liked locally. Nell was pleased with her catch.

Three years passed, and Jim still had not yet proposed to Nell. To her, this was like a slap in the face. All of the other young women her age were either engaged or married, and none of them had courted as long as she and Jim had. She threw hints and pointed out the envious looks of the other young men who would have welcomed being her beau. When none of that moved Jim to propose, Nell decided to take the direct approach.

On the night of November 20, 1901, Nell invited Jim to visit with her at her home for the evening. Nell had arranged it so that she and Jim could sit in the parlor. Sitting there alone with him in conversation, Nell turned the subject toward matrimony. Jim hedged as he always did and Nell lost her patience. It was more than a girl should have to endure, she fumed. Either they were getting engaged or she would refuse to spend any more time with him. She refused to become an old maid waiting for Jim to make up his mind.

Jim became enraged. How dare she give him an ultimatum? He would marry when he was good and ready, but at the same time, he was jealous of the idea of Nell with another man. That idea just made his blood boil. Jim raised his voice and Nell matched him shout for shout. Finally, her family intervened and Mr. Cropsey suggested that Jim go home and cool off. Cropsey was polite but firm in his insistence that the young couple needed space before any more heated words were said.

Jim struggled to contain his anger as Nell escorted him to the porch. Convention dictated that they say a polite goodnight, but the two were both upset. Nell struggled with her own pain. She was livid, and hot tears stung her eyes. The very notion that Jim would not want to marry her broke her heart, for she was truly in love with him. But Nell was also a practical girl, and she was feeling the urge to have a home and family of her own. Jim was upset, too, and he told Nell that they were through. He was breaking off the relationship.

As the couple spoke on the porch, Nell's parents discussed the matter of the fight. Her father felt that Jim was not worthy of Nell. Her mother muttered that Jim probably only had cold feet. Nell's sister, Ollie, had also invited her beau, Roy Crawford, over that evening, and the two had been sitting in another room when the fight had begun in the parlor. They heard Nell and Jim leave the house and heard the couple talking on the porch.

A pall had fallen over the evening and Ollie and Roy decided to call it a night, too. The couple stepped out into the brisk evening air to say goodnight and were a bit surprised that Nell and Jim were nowhere to be seen.

Ollie surmised that Nell had crept back into the house and gone to their room to sulk or cry. She made her way upstairs and stepped into the bedroom expecting to see her sister. The room was empty. Ollie didn't think much of Nell's absence, so she went to bed without giving her sister another thought. Later that night, Ollie awoke and realized that her sister was still gone. She went downstairs and found her father on the back porch eating a snack. He was still unaware that Nell was missing.

Ollie told her father about Nell's absence and the house was roused. The family looked everywhere but there was no sign of her. Before dawn, the family put out an alarm to the neighbors and everyone was looking for Nell.

The family drove themselves to exhaustion in their search. Neighbors and the authorities scoured the area. Jim was questioned and he pled ignorance. He was worried about Nell, too, but he told the authorities that they had broken up on the night that Nell had disappeared. He knew nothing else.

For a month, Nell remained missing. Her family was grieving. Then a letter came, and it confirmed the family's worst fears. It was a confession of sorts. The letter included a map and said that Nell was dead. It said her body could be found at the place marked on the map. For some reason the letter was not taken seriously at first. Perhaps the family was denying the bad news, but at last someone decided to check the spot. Nell's body was found along the Pasquotank River in perfect condition. Despite the fact that she had been missing—and was probably dead—for thirty-seven days, her body looked as if she had passed away only a day or so earlier.

An autopsy revealed that Nell had been struck on the head with a blunt object and that this was the cause of death. All eyes turned toward Jim Wilcox, who became the prime suspect, although there was no concrete evidence against him.

Jim was eventually arrested for the murder and found guilty in 1902. He was sentenced to hang for the murder, but the state Supreme Court overturned the verdict and declared it a mistrial, because of the heavy sentiment against Jim and the fact that there was no evidence to convict him. Jim was then tried again outside the county, and again he was convicted on circumstantial evidence. This time, however, he was sentenced to thirty years. In 1918, he received a pardon from the governor.

Jim became a recluse and committed suicide in 1934. It is said that he contracted with the local newspaper to write a book about what really had happened to Nell, but if so, he never delivered. Uncharitable folks believed that Jim committed suicide because of his guilty conscience. Others said it was because the case ruined his life. Jim always claimed he was innocent.

Those who supported Jim's plea maintained that Roy Crawford should have been considered a suspect, too. It was known locally that he had chosen to date Ollie only because Nell was taken; he had a crush on Nell for some time. Furthermore, Ollie broke off her relationship with Roy shortly after her sister disappeared. Ollie became a recluse herself, and Roy committed suicide a few years later. He left no note to explain his drastic actions.

Nell and Ollie's brother, Will, also died by his own hand in 1913. He left no note to explain his action to his already grief-stricken family.

Shortly after Nell's death, stories began to circulate that she was not resting easy. People began to say that they saw a pretty young woman walking along the water where her body was found. There is no record of Nell haunting Seven Pines during her family's tenure there, but some subsequent owners have claimed to have seen her, both in the house and on the grounds.

A recent owner has a theory about the death of Nell, based upon what his family has experienced and witnessed in the house. According to this theory, Nell was struck and killed accidentally by her father. The family believes that Nell's father mistook the girl for a prowler on the grounds late that same night and shot at her. When the father hurried after the assumed prowler, he found Nell with a head injury. Either Ollie was with him at this time or she discovered the truth shortly thereafter, but this family believes that Ollie shared the secret with her father and that this is why she broke up with Roy and became housebound. The family believes that Nell lingered on in the house or an outbuilding while her father and sister tended her. After a month, she finally perished. That was when the letter was sent so that Nell could be found and have a Christian burial.

Only Nell knows the truth, and she is apparently not giving exact answers to anyone. She is seen in the house, makes sounds, and moves things around, but she has never named her murderer.

A Woman of Conviction

March 10, 1862, was a stressful day for young Emeline Pigott. No one was yet aware of just how long the Civil War would last or how bitter it would be, but everyone was aware that the conflict had come to Morehead City in Crab Point. The townspeople struggled to survive as Union troops scattered throughout the area. Neighbors, old friends, and even families were divided in their loyalties. Many people were Confederate sympathizers but dared not speak of their true loyalties in the Union-occupied area. Others had decided to support the Union forces for financial reasons. Still others truly were Union sympathizers. Emeline Pigott, a petite woman with lush auburn hair, made her own choice, but she kept it private.

Emeline's father took a middle-of-the-road approach, hoping that he and his family might be spared from harm. Emeline, however, secretly took in a wounded Confederate soldier and hid him in the house. There she cared for him. She and her older brother, Levi, had spoken about their own beliefs and she knew that Levi's hot blood boiled when he thought of the Union forces taking over their land.

On the evening of March 10, a neighbor and friend of Emeline's father, Edwin Forsyth, came to call. He was a frequent guest, but Emeline worried about this visit, with the soldier hiding only a few feet from where Forsyth was standing. Emeline quickly called her father, but as the two gentlemen greeted one another, a cough was heard. Emeline immediately began faking a bad cough, and the gentlemen left the hall to tend to her problem.

Emeline felt like a caged animal that night. Her nerves were shot. Despite the fact that Forsyth was a family friend, she did not trust him to keep her secret if she was found out. The Union forces did not look kindly upon those aiding the Confederates, and Emeline was worried about the situation.

As the hours wore on, she slipped away to tend the soldier once more, and then decided that she needed some fresh air to calm her nerves. She pulled a shawl around her shoulders and a scarf over her auburn locks and slipped outdoors. A cool mist filled the air, and Emeline knew she must go back inside, but she could not bring herself do it. Emeline walked aimlessly along and soon found herself at the Newport River. She paused for a moment. Had she heard a sound? Emeline waited but heard nothing. She shook herself and forced herself to be calm. She decided to turn around and return to her home. Then, suddenly, something rushed at her in the darkness and a hand pressed against her mouth, stifling a scream.

She was terrified as she found herself bound by a man's strong arms. "Promise not to scream and I'll let you go," the man hissed urgently. "Are you a Confederate sympathizer?"

Emeline became calm and she nodded. The man released the pressure on her mouth and allowed her to step out of his hold. Emeline turned to see a tall, young man in a long cloak. By the light of the moon, she saw he was a Union naval officer. The young man spoke hurriedly, but she heard the slight lilt of a southern accent.

The officer seemed frightened. "I have family near here at New Bern, ma'am, and I need to get a message to the Confederates. The Union forces are planning to burn Trent River Bridge and attack the town near there. New Bern will be cut off."

Something about this young officer made Emeline trust him. "When will this happen?" she gasped.

The officer shook his head. "A day at most. Our forces will reach the shore at the mouth of Slocum's Creek."

With those words the man melted back into the darkness. Within seconds, Emeline heard splashing and the slap of ores hitting the water. She paused a moment as she considered what to do. Someone had to warn the Confederates, but who—and how?

Emeline turned and stumbled, falling to the ground. Whatever she tripped over was soft, and she groped around for it. She didn't need a light to tell her that it was a body. Had the young officer killed a Union sentry so that he might give his warning?

Emeline turned and raced back toward her home. A great resolve filled her. She decided she would carry the message to the Confederates herself. It would take too much time to locate someone else trustworthy. At the house, she roused the stable boy and ordered him to saddle a fast horse. She hurried inside and changed into riding clothes, leaving a note for her father that said she had gone to visit a friend and would return the next afternoon.

Back in the stable, she mounted her horse and prepared to leave when she felt a restraining hand on her horse's bridle. She looked down into her brother Levi's earnest eyes.

"Where are you going?" he said in a husky tone.

"I'm going off to see Mary Belle. I left a note for Father. He was sleeping and I didn't want to wake him or Mama." The lie came easily to her lips, but Levi was not fooled.

"Where are you really going?" he demanded.

Emeline had no time now for explanations. "I have to hurry now, Levi, but let me go and I'll give you a full accounting upon my return. It's an emergency." Something about her anxiety struck Levi, and he loosed the bridle.

"Godspeed, sister, whatever your errand is. I look forward to a full report upon your return."

Emeline smiled and dug her heels into the horse's flank. She felt a need to hurry.

The journey was long and difficult. Emeline feared she might be discovered by a Union picket before she reached the Confederate lines. She kept her horse in the grass as much as possible to mute the sounds. Several times she smelled campfires and heard voices. Each time, she skirted the areas.

Suddenly, Emeline's horse reared as a man dashed out of the darkness. For one terrible second, Emeline trembled with fear, but then she saw that the young soldier was clad in ragged butternut clothes and she was quickly relieved. She asked the soldier how to reach the Confederate lines. He was dazzled by the beautiful young woman with her urgency and ardent voice and gave her explicit directions to a Confederate camp. Quickly, she went on her way.

When she arrived at the camp forty minutes later, Emeline was stopped by a mounted officer there. She looked into his eyes and saw one of the handsomest men she had seen. Taking hold on the bridle of Emeline's mount, the officer introduced himself as Capt. Stokes McRae.

"What might we do for you young woman?" he asked.

"Please, I must see the commander," Emeline said.

For just a moment, Captain McRae's gray eyes scanned the young woman as though he were assessing her. "I'm sorry but Colonel Taylor is too busy to receive callers currently."

Emeline's eyes flashed. "Sir, he'll see me if he doesn't want his troops routed. I bring important information. Now please, take me to Colonel Taylor." Emeline's voice was strong and commanding, but inside she felt nearly faint. Her tone was impudent in a way that was improper for a well-bred young woman, but the tone impressed Captain McRae. He released the bridle and turned his own mount. "Follow me," he ordered.

Soon, Emeline was face to face with Colonel Taylor. Captain McRae stood in the tent with them and listened as Emeline poured out her strange tale. Colonel Taylor questioned Emeline about the information and made note of it. He was impressed by the bravery of the young woman, but he saw she was tired and needed rest. He ordered sherry and biscuits to revive the girl. As she ate, he and Captain McRae spoke to Emeline of her home and her family. They learned what was happening in Morehead City.

"Miss Pigott, I must commend you upon your bravery. Your journey tonight surely has saved many Confederate lives," Colonel Taylor began. He paused a moment as if he was thinking of a plan. "Under other circumstances, I would never suggest this, but Miss Pigott would you be interested in bringing us further news of Union troop movements?"

Emeline pinned the colonel with her eyes. "You want me to become a spy?" Her voice was incredulous.

"It is only that you are so brave and the movements of a well-bred young woman would not be watched with as much scrutiny as those of a man." The colonel trailed off. "It would be dangerous work. I'll allow you time to think about it."

Emeline was rapidly coming to terms with the idea. "I need no time, colonel," she said smartly. "I would be honored to spy for the Confederacy, but how would I pass information along? I could not make a journey often or it would cause comment."

"There is a Capt. Josiah Pender in Morehead City to whom you could pass information. Do you know the gentleman?" The colonel's voice was excited.

Emeline nodded. "I have met him on occasion."

"Good, pass information to him or any agent he instructs you to. But, Miss Pigott, I must give you one vital piece of advice. Spying is not a school game. It could well lead to your death. Do not ever be caught carrying papers with illicit information or the Union forces will kill you." The colonel's voice was deep with concern.

"They could hang me?" Emeline breathed.

The colonel nodded. "Being a woman is no protection for a spy. They could hang or shoot you, but they will not spare you. Does this change your mind?"

Emeline thought hard for only a moment. "I'll do what I can, but how will I get information? I would not have had any tonight if the young naval officer had not accosted me. We cannot rely upon such circumstances again."

Colonel Taylor shrugged. "I believe that you are a resourceful young woman. Simply keep your ears and eyes open. Look for troop movements, observe if quantities of goods are purchased or men amassed. All tidbits you garner could be helpful." Colonel Taylor turned to Captain McRae. "Stokes, take this young woman back to her home or as close to it as you safely can."

With that the colonel bid Emeline farewell and left her with Captain McRae. Emeline enjoyed her ride home despite her fatigue. Captain McRae was a fascinating man, and she was captivated by his stories and personality. When they reached Calico Creek, he bid her farewell but promised to see her again as soon as possible.

Within days Emeline had taken Levi into her confidence, and the siblings both became spies for the Confederacy. Levi often helped his sister slip away or arrange meetings. She was instructed to give information to several people by Captain Pender. Among them was an old peddler who was selling great quantities of goods to the Union forces, but was doing so only as a cover for his spying operations.

Through the years, Emeline honed her skills as a spy. She volunteered to tend the Confederate prisoners of war at the prison at New Bern. She sewed secret pockets into her petticoats and brought supplies to the prisoners. She kept messages on slips of paper covered in silk and hid them in her elaborate hairstyles. She arranged lavish parties at her home where Union officers succumbed to her charms. One man in particular, Major Allen, grew quite possessive of her. Emeline quickly learned that his tongue was loosed when he walked in the moonlight with her. She allowed him to court her openly as long as he unwittingly gave her information.

Emeline and Captain McRae continued to meet in secret and the two fell in love. Captain McRae was in awe of the brave young woman and she loved his strength and honor. They became engaged and planned to be married after the war ended.

For three years, Emeline and Levi spied for the Confederates by befriending the Union troops. Then, one cold February day in 1865, Emeline was scheduled to drop information with a courier in town.

She stashed a message about troop movements and supply ships in her hair, as she had so many times before. She also filled her secret pockets with supplies for the Confederate prisoners of war she planned to tend to that day.

In town, Emeline walked down the street and waited for the appointed moment to meet the courier. Instead, she saw the peddler who sold supplies to the Union troops. Of late, he had offered up little information, and for a moment, Emeline stopped to watch him. The old man saw her and looked away, refusing to meet her gaze. Money did strange things to people she mused, and she suddenly felt a qualm of fear. She had never been truly comfortable with the peddler and now he made her nervous.

She turned away and pretended to be looking into a shop window when she felt a hand upon her elbow. She turned to find herself facing two Union soldiers. One was an older, coarse man wearing the rank of sergeant; the other was a young corporal, who offered her a reassuring smile. The sergeant spoke first. "Miss Emeline, please come with us. We wouldn't want to make a scene here."

Emeline felt terror clutch her heart. Her mind was whirling fast. Colonel Taylor's words from long ago came back to her. "Do not ever be caught carrying papers with illicit information or the Union forces will kill you." She thought of the paper hidden in her hair.

"Please tell me where you are taking me," she demanded haughtily as she shook her arm loose from the grasp of the squat Union sergeant.

"To the prison at New Bern. I believe you are familiar with it, but this time you'll remain as a guest." There was a sneer in the sergeant's voice.

Emeline's voice was steely. "I'll need to return home first for my personal articles."

"We can't let you go ma'am," apologized the young corporal, "but we could send for your things and notify your folks of what has happened." The corporal's gentleness eased Emeline slightly.

The sergeant snorted in disgust. "Stop being so polite to her," he shouted at the corporal. "She's no lady. She's a spy and she's gotten good Union men killed. She'd kill you, too, if she could." The sergeant's hatred dripped from his voice like poison.

Emeline allowed herself to be escorted to an army wagon, but as she was about to be lifted up onto the seat, a local businessman named Cornelius Hill excused himself and asked the sergeant what was happening. Emeline knew Hill well. He was a merchant who made a great deal of money selling information to both sides through the war years. Now Hill listened in shock as he heard that Emeline was being arrested.

"Sergeant, might I offer my own closed coach," Hill suggested. "For Miss Emeline's consideration, of course."

Emeline was grateful for the gesture. The sergeant could find no way to gracefully refuse the offer. Everyone knew Emeline and certainly it would do the local relations no good if they shamed her needlessly. Hill joined her inside after giving the driver strict instructions on where to go.

At the prison, Emeline felt trapped. She knew she had to destroy the message, but how? She balked at leaving the carriage until the commander came out and told her why she was arrested. The sergeant left her to find the commander, and the corporal stood guard outside the carriage. Quickly, Emeline retrieved the message from her hair and ate it. She had no choice. By the time the commander arrived, she seemed to have changed her mind and was compliant.

A local woman searched Emeline and found the stash in her secret pockets. Emeline was carrying two pairs of pants, a shirt, a pair of boots, toothbrushes, and two pocketknives in her petticoats. The items were reason enough to detain her, but nothing found proved that she was a spy.

Emeline remained in her cell for days. She soon heard that some of the soldiers were plotting to kill her. The sergeant had been rousing the men, and one night they tried to poison her with an overdose of chloroform, but Emeline awoke in time and managed to breathe through a crack in the window until the poison dissipated. Now she feared that her death was imminent. She refused to eat for fear the food was tainted. That same day she convinced the gentle young corporal to take a message to Hill for her. She had formed a plan, but it was a desperate one. It all hinged on her ability to act.

Late that day Hill appeared in her room at the prison. Emeline was hungry and frightened and she poured all her energy into her performance.

"Mr. Hill," she began sweetly. "I find myself in need of your assistance. I understand that you have become good friends with Colonel Rodman who runs the prison. I want to be released before this day is out or I shall tell everyone about your secret deals and the secret deals made by other prominent men in town." Her voice was cool but brooked no arguments.

"I don't know what you're talking of young lady," Hill began, but Emeline could see that he was already rattled.

"I could tell them the names of the fishermen you hired to take supplies to Union blockade runners. I could tell them about the written message on Confederate troop movements that you sent to . . ."

"Stop," commanded Hill in a hoarse whisper. "I'll see what I can do. Only do not tell your tales. They are not true but perhaps someone would believe them and they would not only ruin me, they might get me killed."

"If I were home," Emeline replied. "I'm sure that my memory would fade. I want desperately to forget all of this."

Hill again promised to do his best and then left. Hours stretched on and finally night came. Emeline was hungry, tired, and discouraged. Either the ruse had not worked or Hill was unable to help.

Late that night, a soldier came to tell Emeline to gather her possessions, for she was leaving. Within the hour, she found herself in her father's loving arms. He and Levi had come to take her home.

When the war ended, Emeline waited to hear from Stokes McRae, but no word came. Then one day a young soldier driving a wagon arrived at the house. He told Emeline that he had served under McRae and that he had died at the Battle of Gettysburg. The soldier had revered his commander and was delivering McRae's body to Emeline, along with the truth about her fiancé's fate.

The body was now a skeleton in a tattered uniform. Emeline was unable to see anything that convinced her that the body belonged to Stokes, but she had the bones buried in the family plot with the words UNKNOWN SOLDIER carved in the headstone.

Emeline had faced the entire Union army, but she could not face the loss of Stokes McRae. She grieved for him the rest of her life and requested that she be laid to rest beside the "Unknown Soldier" when she died.

Since her death, people have reported seeing a young woman in Civil War–era garb and a Confederate officer strolling along the lanes near the house and the waters of Calico Creek. Those who first encountered the phantom lovers insisted they were the spirits of Emeline and Stokes reunited for eternity in death.

The Flaming Phantom Ship of Ocracoke Inlet

Each September, locals just off the northern shore of Ocracoke Inlet will tell you to watch for the new moon. On that night, they say, a ship can be seen burning as it slowly drifts by. Those who witness the scene never forget it.

The origin of this story goes far back in European history. In the late 1600s, religious wars ravaged Europe. Among those caught in the crossfire were the German-speaking people of the Palatinate. Thousands of refugees from the region poured into England, along with others from the valley of the Rhine. It was enough to upset the economy there, and it was soon evident to England's Queen Anne that something needed to be done. The refugees, however, were skilled craftsmen, tradesmen, businessmen, and even wealthy nobles, just the sort of productive people the queen wanted as settlers in the English colonies in America. When Swiss-born Baron Christophe DeGraffenried suggested that he should lead the refugees to America, the queen was delighted. She helped to facilitate the acquisition of the ships, and some of the wealthier refugees helped fund the migration to America. Several people made it safely to the Carolina coast, where they began to rebuild their lives. Others followed suit and soon the settlers were a thriving group. When word of the success of the migration reached others back in England and in the Palatinate, more decided to immigrate as well.

A group of wealthy Palatine refugees chartered a ship and set sail to follow their brethren. They managed to take many valuables from their homes, including chests of gold coins, jewelry, silverware, and candlesticks.

The Palatines were thrilled with their decision to leave for America. The crossing was uneventful, but they were unaware that trouble was brewing beneath the surface. The group had kept much of their wealth hidden during the journey, but the captain and his crew ascertained a fair reckoning of the valuables. As the ship approached the coast of Carolina, they fomented a plan to steal the wealth. None of the passengers aboard knew that their captain had once been a pirate. He had been pardoned at the end of Queen

Anne's War, but now the temptation of the gold and jewels awoke the avarice in him.

Ocracoke Inlet was a major port for passengers and goods going farther inland. On the morning when the Carolina coast was sighted, the captain made an excuse to delay the landing. The immigrants gathered on the deck dressed in their finery and hauled out their stashes. It was a fine September day, but the captain trumped up an excuse as to why he was unable to sail into port that day. He promised to have the problem resolved by tomorrow. The passangers returned to their cabins frustrated at the delay, but still excited about beginning their new lives.

That night was dark, because there was a new moon. Some folks stirred and walked the deck, taking in the air and watching the lights of shore. The captain and his men silently approached and strangled them. After their bodies were hidden in the cargo hold, the sailors slipped down to the cabins, where they slew the rest of the men, women, and children aboard the ship. They gathered all the gold and jewels. They pried rings from the dead hands and ripped necklaces from their necks. When they had amassed their plunder, they put off in smaller boats to the shore where the darkness of the night hid them from view. They made more than one trip in order to get all of their blood-bought bounty, but they did slip away unseen.

The captain, realizing the bodies would be found in the morning, returned with the crew and poured coal oil around the bloody ship and set it on fire. The men hurried before the blaze grew too bright and began rowing away. As they moved into the darkness, they turned back to see the blaze. The entire ship was engulfed. The sails, like sheets of flame, fanned out in the breeze.

Then suddenly, the ship began to move. The anchor rope had burned through and the blazing sails caught the wind. At the same moment, a terrible sound reached their ears. The terrified screams of a woman came from the hold of the ship. The men realized that a witness still remained.

Then other cries rang out. It was as if the dead had come to life. The crew continued rowing, but within seconds realized that they, too, were doomed. The loosed ship was literally bearing down on the little boat at full speed. In seconds, the flaming ship struck the boat and sent the crew crashing into the waters.

Many in the crew drowned. Others were picked up by a small craft. The ship burned brightly as it headed out to sea, but then it turned, without anyone at the wheel, and headed back toward the port and the men in the water.

Those who survived confessed and told their terrible tale. The ship, however, vanished. It had somehow turned again and made its way out into the Atlantic. It is said that each year when the new moon comes in September, the flaming ship returns, and the pitiful cries of the dead, unfulfilled in their dreams, can be heard.

Graveyard of the Atlantic

There is an area off the North Carolina coast where the warm waters of the tropics meet the cold waters of the Labrador Current and clash violently. Further complicating matters are sandy shoals that move constantly. Alexander Hamilton, who as a teenager barely survived a trip through these treacherous waters, called the area "The Graveyard of the Atlantic." The nickname was apt, because the waters here have claimed more than two thousand ships since 1526. Many people aboard those doomed ships perished in the twisting currents that meet there.

Through the years, people have returned from the area with reports of floundering ghost ships, but in 1976, a series of events began to play out that led to perhaps the greatest ghost story ever told about the Graveyard of the Atlantic.

It was a dark, rainy night and a pleasure yacht called *Sea Quest* was caught in a storm. The skipper was a well-known engineer from Southern California named John Fielding. Aboard with John were his pregnant wife and small daughter, and he was greatly concerned for their well-being in the ferocity of the storm. A terrible snap caught John's attention. He hurried forward to see what had happened. John was shocked to find that the cable between the mast and the bowsprit had snapped. Then the main cable quickly snapped, too. The damage was severe, for he could no longer control the vessel. His only hope now was to ride out the storm, and that meant that his yacht had to repel the waters dashing against it. John hurried below deck to check out the structural integrity of the hull. If there was water inside, it could well mean the end for him and his family.

Fortunately, the hull was intact and watertight. John hurried to radio an SOS to the Coast Guard at Ocracoke. He was vastly relieved when Chief Robinson assured him that a rescue vessel was being dispatched immediately.

John returned to his little family and reassured them that all was well. Help was on the way. In his own heart, however, he was not so relieved. The yacht was taking a battering and he doubted it would hold out until help arrived.

Then they saw lights wavering into view out of the darkness. Help had arrived, but it was not in the form of the Coast Guard. A large freighter had loomed up out of the darkness and sidled up alongside the yacht. The captain of the freighter talked to John via radio and offered to help. Never in his life had John been so relieved to see someone. Once the Coast Guard was in route, they asked John to verify the position of the two vessels. When the captain of the freighter realized that help was coming, he informed John that he would move on so that the Coast Guard could get into position when they arrived.

The freighter sailed off into the stormy night and John thought no more about it at that time. The Coast Guard arrived and rescued his family. It was only later at the Coast Guard station that John thought once more about the freighter. He asked the radio operator if he could check on its position and let the captain know that the family had made it to safety.

The radio operator looked shocked and asked John to repeat the names of the ship and the helpful captain. John did so and asked what was wrong. The radio operator immediately called his commander who also listened to John's story. The commander told John that he knew of the ship and it indeed had a captain by the name John identified. But it how could it have been that ship? It had gone down in the Graveyard of the Atlantic many years earlier.

Blackbeard's Many Haunts

Edward Thatch, known by some sources as Edward Teach or Edward Drummond, has gone down in history by his more popular nickname—Blackbeard. Probably the most infamous pirate of all time, Thatch did not start his career with that goal. He began his life at sea as a cabin boy on a privateer during Queen Anne's War.

The British government licensed privateers, or private warships, to attack French vessels in the open water. The British privateers collected the cargo for a bounty and confiscated the ship for use in the war. The captured men were typically conscripted, forced to labor, or killed. At the same time, the privateers disrupted supply lines and destroyed the enemy's morale. Privateers took their chances, but the rewards were great.

At the end of the war, many privateers became pirates, including Thatch, who joined with former privateer Capt. Benjamin Hornigold. Hornigold made Thatch captain of a captured ship before deciding to retire and accept amnesty from the British. Thatch, however, had not amassed a fortune, and so he took over Hornigold's fleet.

Thatch captured a state-of-the-art ship from the French and named it *Queen Anne's Revenge*. He outfitted it with the best men and munitions available at the time. In the *Queen Anne's Revenge*, he began to ply his trade in piracy and was very successful at it.

According to legend, Thatch began calling himself Blackbeard after he took on HMS *Scarborough*, a warship of the British navy, forcing it to break off the attack after hours of fighting. His name became infamous all along the East Coast. Blackbeard was a fearsome man. He stood nearly seven feet tall at a time when most men were at least a foot or more shorter. He had a big barrel chest, from which he would roar, sending his men scurrying. A luxuriant black beard covered the lower half of his face and grew all the way down past his waist. He made tiny braids in the beard, tied with red cloth, along with punky matches or fusing woven through it, so that it would burn when he lit it. He also wove it around his head or hat and down past his ears to illuminate his face in a ghastly light. Blackbeard terrified captain and crew when he and his men invaded their ships. He plied the waters from New England to the Caribbean and chose the many islands and inlets of North Carolina as his base because they were good hiding places. North Carolina was also friendly to him.

Blackbeard roamed the Atlantic Ocean like a fearless predator. He pressed into service some of those he captured, but most fell prey to his sadistic nature and were killed. In certain areas of North Carolina, Blackbeard was both a devil and a god. Among the pirates, he was a lord to be envied and revered. At the height of his career in piracy, Blackbeard commanded four ships and three hundred men.

If Blackbeard was said to have a home on land, it would have been Ocracoke Island. Here, Blackbeard helped the local trade by selling his ill-gotten goods, and so the people overlooked his indiscretions. He built a home on the island that was dubbed Blackbeard's Castle, where he sorted his treasure, threw parties, and rested easily, for no one would dare take on Blackbeard in his castle.

For a time Blackbeard owned a house that is today called Hammock House. One night, he held a party that would go down in history. He invited a young woman whose affections he sought. The woman was amenable because Blackbeard was a powerful man, but during the party the alcohol flowed freely and soon many of his men became drunk. Though none of them would have dared look at the woman for fear of Blackbeard's wrath, one of the crew got drunk enough to become bold. He asked the woman to dance and she obliged him. Noticing them, Blackbeard immediately drew his sword and lunged at the couple. The sailor turned to run, but Blackbeard caught up to him on the stairs and beheaded him. It is said that even today the bloodstains remain on the stairs, and they cannot be removed. On another occasion, Blackbeard sought the affections of a young woman in another port town. This girl, however, was in love with an honest sailor. She gave her young man a ring that was a family heirloom for him to wear while out at sea. By his own luck, Blackbeard captured the sailor's ship and recognized the ring when he saw it on the man's finger. He knew exactly what it meant and where it had come from. Furious that he had been slighted, Blackbeard had the man's hand cut off and sent it back to the woman who had spurned him. The sailor was then killed. When the young woman opened the "gift" and found her betrothed's hand and ring, she passed out. She never recovered from the shock and died shortly afterward.

Teach's Hole is a spot still marked on maps today. It was here that Blackbeard and his first mate, Israel Hand, were drinking below decks one night. Blackbeard pulled out a pistol and blew out the single nubbing candle that lit the murky darkness. "I'll shoot anyone who does not run," he announced in a drunken slur. Hand did not believe his trusted captain would harm him, so he continued to drink. The others in the room wisely ran off. Blackbeard aimed the gun in the direction of his friend and shot him. Hand was forever crippled by his friend and master, but he continued to serve him for years afterward.

Eventually, Blackbeard longed for a normal life. In 1716, he married a sixteen-year-old girl named Mary Ormand in the port town of Bath and built a home at Plum Point near Bath Creek. (Blackbeard allegedly had wives in several port towns, including a young woman he installed at Teach's Castle, as well as mistresses from New England to South Carolina. In all, Blackbeard was said to have twelve wives in America and a wife, to whom he had a son, in England.)

At Plum Point, Blackbeard lived across from the home of Tobias Knight, assistant to Gov. Charles Eden. According to legend, Blackbeard bribed Governor Eden for a pardon. Blackbeard abused his young wife and held terrible parties that shamed her. The town was terribly upset, but no one wanted to take him on. Soon his fortune was squandered on women, alcohol, and parties, and he decided that it was time to take to the Atlantic again. He purchased a ship he named *Adventure* and pretended to be an honest sailor. Within months, though, he was openly pirating. This breach of his pardon would eventually lead to his capture and death by beheading.

One night in November 1718, Blackbeard threw a drunken party at Teach's Hole. He and his men were in no shape to fight, but the people of Ocracoke Island had always protected him before, and Blackbeard felt comfortable there. It was there that his ship was spotted by British lieutenant Robert Maynard, who commanded two sloops searching for Blackbeard. The sloops slid silently into place that night and waited for orders. Virginia governor Alexander Spotswood had placed a price on Blackbeard's head and had promised to bring the menace to an end. Blackbeard was so successful that he was biting into the revenue of honest shipping companies and the British Crown had ordered him arrested or killed.

At dawn, two skiffs were sent out to determine how best to approach the pirate's ship, but when Blackbeard's men saw the skiffs, they opened fire. Blackbeard hoped only to escape, but Maynard had every intention of bringing the pirate in dead or alive. Maynard pulled an ingenious maneuver when he ordered his men below deck and made his ship appear to be disabled. Blackbeard thought he had won and, along with his men, boarded the ship.

Suddenly, they found themselves confronted with a large force of men armed with guns and swords. A pitched battle ensued, and soon Maynard stood face-to-face with Blackbeard. Maynard fired, creasing Blackbeard's temple. Blackbeard lunged forward, and a marine swung his sword down across Blackbeard's neck, nearly severing his head. Blackbeard glared with fiendish hate and fought on with Maynard. The two men sparred with swords for several minutes. Maynard inflicted several more wounds, but Blackbeard still came on. At last, Blackbeard pulled a pistol from his belt, leveled it at Maynard, and then fell forward on his face. He was dead at last. Later, it was learned that Blackbeard had been shot once and stabbed thirty-seven times. His head was lopped off and placed securely on the bow of Maynard's sloop, *Ranger*. What eventually happened to the head is not known, although records indicate that it was still attached to the sloop when it reached Virginia. In a strange twist of fate, Blackbeard had been attempting to get a pardon from King George I, and the pardon did make it to North Carolina, but not until one month after his death. This second pardon had also been obtained with the help of his friend, Governor Eden.

Today, there are those who say that they have seen Blackbeard still sailing along Ocracoke Island in *Queen Anne's Revenge* or the *Adventure*. On other occasions, the lights from his ship are seen floating by. Those who know about such things will tell you that it is none other than Blackbeard. Others say that Blackbeard can be seen swimming around in Teach's Hole. The pirate has also been spotted decapitated, searching for his head that was severed in his last battle. This is not a ghost that anyone should wish to see, for it is said that bad luck befalls those who witness him.

It is believed that Blackbeard did hide a vast treasure that has never been found, but the price for finding it may be too steep. If someone is brave enough to risk the bad luck and can follow the ship or ghost lights to where they stop, then Blackbeard's great treasure will be theirs, if Blackbeard allows them to take it. He never was a man who shared well.

The Tragic Spirit of Theodosia Burr

Theodosia Burr was a most unusual young woman. She was the only child of Aaron Burr, vice president of the United States under Thomas Jefferson. Burr was a restless man, prone to making political enemies. His greatest enemy became Alexander Hamilton, whom he killed in a duel. Burr made enemies in high places, and he was eventually brought down on charges of treason for allegedly attempting to create a monarchy in the American West.

Through all of his misadventures, his staunchest supporter was his daughter Theodosia. She and her father had a particularly special relationship. Burr doted on his daughter, but did not allow her to be idle. He personally supervised her education, ensuring that she was as well-educated and well-spoken as any young man. The beautiful Theodosia was courted by the wealthy politician Joseph Alston of South Carolina, later to be governor of the state. The couple married, and Theodosia began a new life in South Carolina, but she never wavered in her support and love for her father.

After his acquital in the teason trial, Burr left the United States for Europe with a heavy heart. He missed Theodosia a great deal in the four years he was gone and wrote to her frequently.

Alston, by then governor of South Carolina, could see the pain that Theodosia suffered living at such a distance from her father, and when she came to him with a plan to visit her father, he agreed to it. Plans were made for Theodosia to sail to New York on a private boat. There she would meet another ship carrying her father and together they would sail back to Europe, where she would visit for a time. Governor Alston made every provision for his wife's safety and comfort. He bid her a fond farewell and embraced her. Theodosia began her journey with the highest of expectations. She was jubilant in the knowledge that she would once again see her father, but her joy turned to fear within hours. According to some reports, pirates boarded the vessel near North Carolina's Bald Head Island and killed all aboard except for Theodosia. The pirates dragged her on deck to face their leader. Theodosia was not the sniveling, pleading woman the pirates might have expected. She was calm in her fear. She faced the pirate captain calmly as he threatened her with death.

"I am not afraid," she told him. "If I am to die by your hand, it will be without so much as a single tear shed."

The pirate captain was impressed by the courage of this beautiful, aristocratic woman. He learned her identity and was even more impressed. This was not the pampered, spoiled rich girl he had imagined her to be. This woman had strength, dignity, and courage. He decided to keep her alive.

He put Theodosia ashore on Bald Head Island under the guard of a crewman. After sinking the ship, he warned the crewman to keep a close eye on Theodosia, for he would return the next day after hiding his ill-gotten bounty.

Theodosia's night on Bald Head Island was terribly unpleasant. She feared for her life and her virtue. She knew that the pirates must kill her at some point to silence her tongue. She watched the crewman as he drank. The dirty man stank of sweat and cheap alcohol. Rum left a sweet smell underlying his filth. After a few hours, he grew drowsy and passed out.

Theodosia watched carefully as her captor became drunk. She tried to figure out a way to save herself. She had no ship to sail in, nowhere to hide, and could not fight off an entire crew of pirates, even if she could manage to kill this one man. No, in the morning the captain would return—and with his return would be pain, degradation, and a death she did not want to suffer. Grimly, quietly, Theodosia had come to a decision. She could not be victorious over the pirates, but she could take their victory from them.

She stood up and quietly made her way down the beach and into the water. Her drunken guard did not witness her end, but Theodosia allowed the waters of the ocean to fill her lungs. When the pirates returned, the captain was furious to find their captive gone and sent the hungover crewman to search for her. Theodosia's body was never found. All that remained of her were footprints that led into the water and a ribbon from her hair that was found in the surf.

For many years, no one knew what had happened to Theodosia. Her husband and father attempted to learn her fate, but there was no sign of this beloved woman or the ship she was last seen boarding. Years later, a couple of pirates came forward and told the story of Theodosia. They claimed to have been aboard the pirate ship that captured her.

For many years, a beautiful young woman in period clothes has been seen walking along the beach and into the surf on Bald Head Island. Many have speculated that this is the beautiful and tragic Theodosia Burr Alston reliving her last moments before she left the mortal world.

The Sanderling Screamer

The beautiful, sandy Outer Banks call to people and invite them to enjoy the waters of the Atlantic Ocean. But these waters are not as gentle as they seem, for lurking close to shore are sharks. On what is known locally as the Sanderling Beach, in the early morning hours, some people have been startled by screams coming from the water. The sound is someone yelling "Shark!" Alarmed by what seems to be a horrible attack, the witnesses run to the water, but they see no one. Still the sounds are real enough to incite them to get help.

On several occasions, the authorities have arrived and searched for signs of the swimmer, but they never find anything. Some locals speculate that the screams are from the ghost of a man who met his end during a shark attack years ago. They believe that no one was around during the attack to render aid and now the spirit of that man is reliving his last desperate struggle for survival over and over again.

The Inner Coastal Plain

THE LEAST POPULATED AREA OF NORTH CAROLINA IS THE RURAL INNER Coastal Plain. This is farm country, and in many respects little ever really changes here. The Devil is known to stalk this land, once showing himself to a minister name Glendinning. This is also the region where a strange phenomena occurs called "spook lights." In two different areas, these light shows dazzle and terrify the observer. Travel this haunted land at your own risk.

The Murderous Spirit

The old cliché, "what goes around comes around," is all too often true. One young slave woman in Pender County, at least, found that it would determine her fate.

Old Jo was a beloved member of her master's family on a plantation in Pender County. She had worked in the house her whole life and helped raise the entire family. When Old Jo grew too old to work, she was given a cabin in the slave section, and a young woman was taken from the fields to help her out. The young woman, Sissy, was told to care for Old Jo. She was to cook, fetch water, and clean for the old woman who could not even walk anymore.

For Sissy, it was a much better life than that of a field slave. Rather than toiling in the hot sun, she worked in the shade of the cabin and all she had to do was give good care to Old Jo.

51

Old Jo knew that the master meant well when he assigned Sissy to care for her, but she was not happy with the girl. The girl had way too much sass in her. Sissy seemed to think that being moved out of the fields meant that she really did not have to work at all, and she did the bare minimum. She would fetch water only when she herself was thirsty. She kept the old woman in bed all day rather than move her into a chair. She fed the old woman what was left after she herself ate.

Old Jo was too ill to help herself or walk to the main house to talk to the master. When some of her friends came to call, she freely told them about the abuse and neglect that she was enduring at Sissy's hands. The older woman would shake with anger and hiss, "If I were younger, I'd slap that girl until the life was out of her."

For months, Sissy allowed Old Jo to suffer needlessly. Jo tried to get word to the master, but then she learned that he and his family had gone on a trip. Now the overseer was in charge, but Old Jo was unable to get word to him either. Again and again, Old Jo threatened to "slap the life out of Sissy."

At last, one evening the overseer found Sissy waiting for him at the edge of the fields. She was obviously upset and she told him that Old Jo had died. The girl insisted that she lay out the body herself. The overseer allowed the girl to do it, because he assumed that she just wanted to do this last act of kindness for the old woman with whom she had spent so much time. In truth, others knew that it was because she did not want anyone to discover the extent of her neglect.

After the funeral, Sissy went back to Old Jo's cabin and locked herself inside. The overseer sent for Sissy to return to the fields that day, but Sissy refused. She refused to leave the cabin until her master told her to do so.

The next day, the overseer was furious when the girl did not appear with the other workers. He went to the cabin and pounded on the door. No one answered. In a fit of anger, the overseer kicked in the door. Much to his surprise, Sissy was on the floor. A look of fear was frozen on her face, and it appeared as if she had been clawing at the door to get out. She had bruises on her face and her eyes were swollen as if she had taken a beating. The slaves crowded in to see the body. Many of them turned away as it was removed.

The overseer could not explain how the healthy young woman had come to die in the locked cabin, but some of the slaves knew. Old Jo said over and over that she wanted to slap that girl dead. No one ever spoke about it to the overseer or the master, but they knew that Old Jo came back for revenge.

Thalian Hall's Spectral Cast and Crew

Thalian Hall has been a center of entertainment for the people of Wilmington ever since the theater was completed in 1858. Designed by John Montague Trimble and named for Thalia, the Muse of comedy and idyllic poetry, it originally served as a cultural center and opera house. From 1860 to 1932, Thalian Hall was leased to private interests that produced shows in the nationally acclaimed theater. During those years, many notable headliners and famous players trod the boards of the theater, from John Phillip Sousa to Lillian Russell and Buffalo Bill Cody. Throughout the years, there have been several changes made to Thalian Hall. It was redesigned, wired for electricity, and restored to its original appearance after a small fire in 1973. Since 1963, it has been run by the Thalian Hall Center for the Performing Arts, and it continues to host a regular schedule of shows and performances.

Perhaps not all the actors at Thalian Hall are of the living variety, however. Two ghosts reportedly seen there on multiple occasions are those of James O'Neill and Maude Adams. The spirits never shared the stage in life, but they seem content to do so in death.

James O'Neill, father of playwright Eugene O'Neill, performed at Thalian Hall in 1902. He was considered one of the finest actors of his day. Those who work at the theater, though, will tell you that O'Neill's spirit is a prankster. He enjoys disconcerting his human counterparts. For example, workmen have complained that their tools disappear and are later found in unusual spots, or the tools are returned to the same spot after long searches for them.

Another favorite prank of O'Neill's is to mess with the lighting during a show. On multiple occasions, O'Neill has been blamed for randomly turning the dimmer switches up and down and flipping the lights on and off. He has been known to pull down one of the seats in the theater to take in the show during rehearsals, and has been spotted doing so several times.

Actress Maude Adams loved her time playing at Thalian Hall, beginning in 1912. Many believe that she is a protective spirit watching over the venerable old theater and its shows. In something as intricate as a theatrical production, there are many things that can go wrong, and the staff and actors sense that Maude oversees things and keeps the shows going on. She has been sighted a few times, walking along in a black dress.

Costumes changes can be a problem for actors. Quick changes are often required. Years ago, a young actress who needed to do so was sidetracked and forgot to get her costume at the appropriate spot behind stage. The wardrobe assistant also neglected to have it pressed and prepared for the scene. The assistant quickly ran for the dress, but could not find it in the dressing room. When she located it in the actress's dressing room, she was shocked to see it had been prepared. She immediately placed the dress where the actress expected it and heaved a sigh of relief. The assistant assumed the actress had taken care of the dress and profusely thanked her for the unexpected help. The actress was shocked and said she had nothing to do with it. The wardrobe assistant queried others about the dress, but no one took credit for helping. Some folks claim that Maude Adams took care of the details on that particular night.

There is at least one other spirit who haunts Thalian Hall. This is the spirit of a young man who worked at the box office long ago. He is apparently still selling tickets and counting receipts. Like Maude Adams, he, too, seems to be keeping the place in order.

The Pactolus Light

North Carolina has more than its share of strange haunted lights. It is a phenomenon that is found all throughout the state.

Near Greenville is the small town of Pactolus. One evening in early 1900, a young man was riding his horse along the train tracks toward the station.

Hiding near the station were three hoodlums who spotted the man's fine horse. They thought that they may be able to make some good money on it if they stole it and sold it. When the man stepped off the horse, one of the thugs struck him from behind, killing him. The terrified horse reared up, pulling its reins from the hand of the thug who had grabbed them, and ran off. In the darkness, the bandits quickly hid the man's body in the nearby woods.

The horse eventually returned to its stable in Greenville, where the young man's family found it. They became terribly worried when they saw the horse, for they knew well that the young man would never have let it go without a fight. The boy's father immediately set out for the train station, where he questioned folks about his son. No one had seen him in the train station, either buying a ticket or boarding a train. He had simply vanished. The family began a search, but their son was nowhere to be found.

Only days after the young man's disappearance, a few people reported seeing a single light moving along the side of the train tracks each evening. The light came from the direction the boy was riding that fateful day. It often appeared at waist height, which was said to mean the man was walking his steed. When it appeared higher, he was reliving his last ride. Then the light would float off and fade away. It is believed that the young man haunted the same path along the old railroad bed, so that his fiancée would know he did not leave her voluntarily. Today, the tracks are gone and the railroad bed is on private property, but some people say that the light still appears from time to time.

The Maco Lights

There is perhaps no other story of strange lights better documented than the ghostly tale behind the old Maco Railroad Station.

When the Atlantic Coast Line Railroad set to work rebuilding its lines after the Civil War, the company not only improved what existed but also added several new stations. One of those was the small Maco Station in the area known as Farmer's Turnout. In 1867, a series of events occurred there that have made the station famous.

Joe Baldwin was a conductor for the Atlantic Coast Line Railroad, and he took his job very seriously. He spent a great deal of his time in the coach car, where he carried out many of the duties of his job. One night, he was sitting in the rear coach when he noticed his car was not picking up speed. It was soon evident to him that his car had somehow uncoupled from the rest of the train and was slowing to a standstill on the tracks. Joe stuck his head out into the cool night and was horrified to see a faint distant light. Another train was coming along the track just behind him. If that train was not warned, it would slam into the uncoupled car and derail the train. It could be devastating.

Joe grabbed the signal lantern and ran for the little platform that faced the oncoming train. He began to wildly wave the lantern, hoping to get the engineer's attention.

The train bore down on poor Joe, but he held to his post and continued waving frantically as the train narrowed the distance between them. The engineer either never saw the lantern or was not paying attention, for the train never slowed down. But Joe stayed there, waving his lantern until the impact.

The train car was totally destroyed, and poor Joe Baldwin was decapitated. His crushed body was found in the wreckage and his head had landed nearby.

Later, a witness said that Joe never wavered. He stood frantically signaling until just seconds before the crash. At that point, the lantern flew from Joe's hand and landed upright, illuminating the scene with an eerie glow.

Not long after the tragic accident, people reported seeing two strange lights along the railroad tracks at Maco Station. The lights were as bright as a low-wattage incandescent light bulb and came barreling at each other along the tracks. They met and winked out. The lights always appeared about three feet above the left rail of the old track bed. Nothing seemed to make the lights veer from their chosen course.

Through the years, many theories have been offered to explain the lights. The most common is they are refractions from cars passing on the highway. Oddly, however, the first known report of the Maco Lights came in 1873, long before the current highway was built; in fact, those sightings predate the automobile. The other common explanation is ball lightning, although the phenomenon rarely recurs frequently in the same place. Since the lights are seen often—and always above the left rail of the tracks—it seems that ball lightning is only a remote possibility.

The lights seem to have minds of their own and will sway down the tracks until someone approaches them. Then they wink out, only to reappear farther up the tracks or behind the person attempting to get close to them. If left alone, the lights will approach people and then speed backwards away from them. There seems no rhyme or reason to how the lights behave. On occasion, the lights will not appear for some time, and then at other times, they make an appearance every night for weeks. Nothing is known to affect the lights. Neither weather nor celestial events seem to have an impact. Sometimes only one light is seen.

When an earthquake struck in 1886, the lights failed to appear. Eventually, one returned, and for a time people were treated to the rare sight of the original two lights barreling at each other and then winking out. As suddenly as it came, the second light disappeared. Those who have seen the Maco Lights say that they always appear small but grow until they are about the size of an old railroad signal lantern. Other people have reported seeing the decapitated Joe in one of the lights, walking along, searching for his severed head.

Today, it is popular for folks to drive out and look for the Maco Light. The site is a known tourist attraction, and many people who make the journey get to see the light. By now thousands of people have seen the lights and not a single explanation has successfully explained away this mystery. Perhaps the most famous person to witness the strange phenomena was President Grover Cleveland, who viewed the lights while his presidential coach stopped there to take on fuel. He went away as puzzled as everyone else.

The railroad had to acknowledge the fact that the lights exist. In the Maco area, the railroad signalmen used red and green lights, so that engineers could distinguish the signals from the Maco Light and avoid accidents. Even with that precaution, there were many instances where trains were slowed down or stopped because the engineer saw the light and was not sure what it meant.

Perhaps it is just a simple ghostly phenomenon. Maybe poor Joe Baldwin really is still trying to signal that train from long ago to stop before it is too late.

The Spirits of Camp Lejeune

Camp Lejeune is a Marine Corps base, named for Lt. Gen. John Archer Lejeune, commander of the Marine Corps during World War I. The base incorporates more than fourteen miles of beachfront property and is considered the best training facility in the world for amphibious operations. Through more than sixty-five years of service, tens of thousands of marines have gone through training at Camp Lejeune. During those years, a small number of marines have reported strange events occurring there.

Campsite 12 was the scene of perhaps one of the most interesting paranormal events at Camp Lejeune. On a cold and damp November night in 1977, a platoon was camping in the forest, preparing for war games. Late that night, the commander instructed four men in the platoon to go forward in a reconnaissance patrol. It was the understanding of this patrol that the remainder of their platoon would follow approximately one hour behind them.

The patrol had been moving forward for roughly twenty minutes when they suddenly halted. The point man motioned, indicating that he saw troop movements ahead. The young marines assumed that they were now participating in war games and assumed ambush positions. In the darkness, nothing seemed to move for nearly fifteen minutes, as the men strained to catch some sign of the troops before them. Suddenly, they were shocked to find movement in the trees above them. Voices seemed to come from nowhere and surround them. The men struggled to make out the enemy but saw no one. The radio operator immediately contacted the lieutenant and requested a confirmation that they were alone at the site. The lieutenant checked his information and confirmed that no one should be in the woods. The lieutenant then ordered the men to observe the action going on around them and report back to him. What the men claimed to see were Civil War soldiers in pitched battle. Indeed, that land did see combat during the war, but the men who reported the strange events had no idea about it. In fact, there have been other scattered reports of Civil War soldiers moving through the woods. It seems that the Marine Corps is sharing its land with the restless dead of the North Carolina's past.

The Devil and Glendinning

For some strange reason, the Devil seems to fancy North Carolina. The Prince of Darkness figures prominently in the legends and folk tales of the Tar Heel State. One particular man, according to one story, was plagued by the Devil for quite some time. Although it sounds like a local legend, there are folks who are convinced of its truth, for the man who told the tale was none other than Reverend William Glendinning, an eighteenth-century preacher from Halifax County. Reverend Glendinning was a respected clergyman, and he kept a written record of his encounters.

In autumn of 1785, Glendinning was traveling through the northeastern section of the state. He was boarding at the home of the John Hargrove family on a cold November night when some neighbors came calling. It was shortly after Glendinning had spoken on the subject of the Devil at that evening's church meeting. The men wanted to know more. Glendinning delivered further discourse on the topic, when he suddenly paused and warned that the Devil could visit any man. In fact, he believed that the Devil would be calling on the Hargrove house soon.

The stunned family and neighbors paused, not sure how to continue. An impending visit by Satan is certainly something that deserves contemplation and trepidation. Following the lull in the conversation caused by Glendinning's startling announcement, there was a knock at the door. The reverend seemed to be the only one with the presence of mind to answer it, and so he arose. At the door stood a creature, which Glendinning later described to be "black as coal—his eyes and mouth as red as blood, and long white teeth gnashed together." The reverend closed the door against the beast, and as the door crashed shut, a terrible storm suddenly erupted. Rain lashed the structure, while hurricane winds ripped windows, causing them to rattle in their frames. It was as if a fury came out of the darkness to try and gain entry inside. It took a moment for everyone, including Glendinning, to regain their composure.

Throughout the following months, the poor Hargrove family was horrified to find that the Devil was determined to gain entrance to their home. At least two or three times a week Old Spark appeared and pounded at the door. The family always shut him out, praying for him to go away.

One night, Glendinning was again boarding with the Hargrove family when he answered the door and once again found himself nose-to-nose with the Devil. The reverend again slammed the door and shortly thereafter retired for the night. The wind blew and snow fell. In his room, Glendinning heard a voice calling from outside. He looked out the window to see the Devil's face pressed close to

the window pane. From outside came a loud voice that seemed to reach the corners of the house. "Oh, that there was but mercy for the wretch that blasphemes the Holy One of Israel," the voice cried out. It sounded like a man, but Glendinning knew better. He told the Hargrove family to beware the voice, and it was gone as suddenly as it had come.

For several months thereafter, the voice and image of the Devil seemed to have disappeared from the house, and the Hargrove family once again resumed a normal life. On another visit to the house, Glendinning was entreated by the children to accompany them to a nearby field. It was spring and the day was pleasant, so the reverend tagged along. As he spoke with the children, he noticed a figure coming toward them. As it drew closer, Glendinning instructed the children to get behind him. The figure was clearly seen in the afternoon light and it was not human. It was the Devil once more, bent on accosting Glendinning. He described it as "upward of five feet high, round the top of his head there seemed to be a ridge; some distance under the top of his head there seemed a bulk, like a body, but bigger than any person; about 15 or 18 inches from the ground there appeared something like legs, and under them feet; but no arms or thighs. The whole as black as any coal . . . his mouth and eyes as red as blood."

The children huddled in fear, but Glendinning prayed and the figure vanished. Still the Devil was not yet done with the minister. In 1786, Glendinning took up residence in a cabin on a farm near the Hargrove property. That summer the Devil seemed to delight in tormenting him, appearing often in the orchard near the cabin and making a long, spiked horn emerge from his head. The reverend rebuked the Devil and called upon the name of the Lord to cast him out. The Devil would then grow weak and shake. According to Glendinning's account, fireballs would explode from his eyes and he would stagger back as if driven by the words that Glendinning spoke. Then he would disappear.

A year of visitations had now gone by and poor Glendinning was feeling the worse for the experience. He knew the Devil was after his soul, but he continued to minister. Eventually the Devil gave up and left him alone.

All of this probably would have been forgotten if not for the fact that Glendinning played a role in the spread of the Methodist

Church in the new nation. He wrote about his experiences, including his encounters with the Devil, in an autobiography, *The Life of William Glendinning, Preacher of the Gospel*, published in Philadelphia in 1795. Had a less respected man told this tale, it surely would not have been believed.

The Beast of Bladenboro

January 4, 1954, was a typical winter's day in Bladenboro, but for some local folks it would be the first of many days of terror. Three dogs were killed that night. They were not shot or hit by cars or poisoned; their skulls were crushed and chewed. Near the bodies there were footprints larger than a man's hand. Folks argued that the tracks were those of a big cat, while others insisted that a canine made them. There were some reports that a dairy goat was also found dead in a similar fashion.

The next morning, January 5, the story of the three dogs and their strange demise made the front page of the local paper. Something large was out there killing domestic pets and livestock, and people were afraid. Anything large enough to kill a goat, hog, or young cattle was large enough to kill a human. Besides, at least one of the dogs that had been killed was large and known to be aggressive. How had any creature gotten close enough to crush its head and chew it? And what about those oversized footprints found nearby?

By the next morning, a panic was spreading and people were pressing the local police chief to do something. He decided to take three coon hounds to the site to let them get the scent. He then turned them loose. To everyone's shock, the hounds refused to follow the scent. Whatever was out there, the hounds wanted no part of it. That only unnerved folks more. They wondered what could be in those woods that had frightened the dogs so badly.

The Wilmington newspapers had a field day with the story. The chief released the details of a necropsy on the dogs that had been killed the previous day. According to the Wilmington *Morning Sun* of January 5, 1954, he said one of the dogs was "opened up today. And there wasn't more than two or three drops of blood in him." The paper continued, "In all three cases, the victims' bottom lip had been broken open and his jawbone smashed back."

The reports that the animals had been drained of their blood had the town bandying around words like monster, vampire, and bloodlust. They speculated on what kind of animal smashes the head of a dog flat and then sucks out the blood.

People grew more afraid. So far the beast was blamed for killing three dogs, a goat, a couple calves, and three pigs, but it had stayed away from humans. People came into town insisting that they had seen the beast moving about their properties, but the descriptions were vague. Eyewitnesses claimed that it was large, and estimates ran from 90 pounds to 150 pounds. The figure was either dark or black or tabby. It was catlike or canine depending on the witness. One thing that all informants agreed on was that the beast made a cry like a woman in pain. It was hair-raising and kept people indoors at night. Men had taken to carrying guns and children were no longer let out to play. Bladenboro was a town under siege, but the monster stalking them was a mystery.

The radio picked up the story and big-game hunters came in from all over. At the zenith of the events nearly one thousand men were in the woods hunting the beast. They came armed with pistols, shotguns, big-game rifles, and traps. It was amazing to watch the tiny town of one thousand people double in weeks. The men slogged across four hundred acres of swampland, known locally as Green Swamp, looking for what was now dubbed the Beast of Bladenboro. Hunters came with bear dogs, trackers, and every gadget they could think of. Amazingly, the only known casualty of this hunting frenzy was a bicycle that was mutilated by a local farmer when he got monster fever. No one was injured and that was a miracle in itself.

Locals now speculated that the beast was anything from a bear to a monster mountain lion. Recent speculation has added alien monster let loose on humanity and government experiment gone badly to the list of possibilities.

On January 6, 1956, a young mother was on her front porch at about 7:30 P.M. when a large, vicious dog came out of nowhere after her. The woman locked herself in the house and called for help. A large cat-like print was found in her yard. The story was duly reported the following day in the paper. The press stated that the "beast stalked toward her." Whether this had anything to do with the Beast of Bladenboro was never really ascertained. In this carnival atmosphere, it only added to the mix. Now, the hunters felt justified in trying to kill the beast because it had gone after a human being.

The newspapers advised that children should not be let out to play. Beloved pets were taken inside at night to prevent the beast from killing them. In only two days, six dogs were found dead and one was literally dragged away and never found.

By January 7, another dog was killed. No one had any doubts that something had to be done. The police chief came up with the idea of tying several dogs up in Green Swamp as bait and watching them until something came after them. The mayor vetoed that idea. He felt that with so many hunters out, someone was bound to be shot and that would not be good for him at reelection time.

At this point, the newspapers and radio stations weren't the only ones making money off the Beast of Bladenboro. The mayor owned a movie theater in town, and he began to advertise, "Now you can see the cat. We've got him on our screen . . . The Big Cat, all day Saturday, January 9." On January 13, a bobcat was caught and maimed in a steel trap. The hunter who set the trap shot the beast. The town officials were unsure if they should rejoice or not, however, because the bobcat was certainly too small to fit the descriptions, and its feet were too small to fit the tracks. But many folks wanted it to be the beast and some even had photos taken with it.

The next day, a young hog was found dead with a flattened skull and no blood in its body. It was the sign of the Beast of Bladenboro, no doubt, but it would be his last kill in the small town. Over the years, domestic pets and small livestock in other towns in North Carolina have fallen victim to a presumed creatures, but never so many in such a short time as in Bladenboro. The mystery of what happened there in those few days in 1954 lingers on.

Eastern Piedmont

EASTERN PIEDMONT PROVINCE IS KNOWN AS THE FALL LINE, OR THE area where the topography changes from coastal to upland characteristics. In North Carolina, this area contains the state's more populated regions. The largest cities are located here, and they are rich with colorful history. Raleigh, the state capital, is a most haunted area, with many ghosts in the Capitol and Governor's Mansion. The region is rich in Civil War lore, and the ghostly denizens of that conflict are more urbane. Yet the sheer number of ghostly tales should impress anyone who dares to look into this darker side of the Eastern Piedmont's colorful past.

The Whatever You Call It

In the spring of 2004, Bill and Gayle Kurdian, an Asheboro couple, set up their infrared-sensitive game camera, hoping to capture the image of a strange beast that they had seen around their home. Before long, the camera captured what they wanted— a long-tailed, fox-eared canine, with a slim body similar to that of a jackal. The creature was about eighteen inches long from nose to rump. Its back end appeared slightly higher than its front end. The beast slinked along silently with a cat-like movement. The problem is that no such creature is known to exist in the Asheboro area.

There is no denying that something strange visited the Kurdian home. The family had been putting food out to feed the local wildlife when they first saw the creature. It came along with a fox and was eating corn one night when it was first sighted. Since then it was seen multiple times at the feeding area. The family has observed the creature long enough to notice changes. They have determined it is a female who is nursing pups, though the young have not been spotted.

The Kurdians contacted the local zoos as soon as they saw the creature. There had been no reports of anyone missing an exotic pet, and none of the curators could identify the beast. There is speculation that the beast is a hybrid. One curator suggested that it was a fox with parasites, but there is no known animal that resembles the beast the Kurdians captured on film.

After the Kurdians' photograph appeared in the *Courier-Times*, people began to contact the paper to say that they had seen the beast, too. Since the story made the national news and the Internet, tens of thousands of people have responded. People in New York, Virginia, Ohio, and Oregon have contacted news Web sites to state that they have seen a similar creature in their areas. Whatever you want to call it, this beast remains a mystery for the people of Asheboro.

The Legend of Peter Dromgoole

Most universities and colleges have a ghost story or two to tell. The tale of poor Peter Dromgoole has come down through the years from the University of North Carolina. Peter Dromgoole was a very lucky young man. He came from a wealthy family in Virginia, and so he bore a name that opened doors for him. He was a handsome man who could charm the ladies, and so he was popular. He had no financial worries and saw his future as secure and bright. To further ensure his good fortune, Peter applied to the University of North Carolina in 1831. He failed to pass his admissions test, and so he hired a tutor and lingered on at Chapel Hill, presumably to take the test again once he had studied more. Peter, however, was unable to see the real value of an education, and he became distracted. There were parties where alcohol flowed freely. There were young ladies everywhere. Peter indulged in both. Despite his lack of commitment, Peter did eventually get into school. For two years, he continued his deleterious ways until he met a young woman named Fanny.

Fanny was not from his social class, but she was a good young woman who was upright and moral. She caught his attention at first because she was breathtakingly lovely. But after speaking with her, Peter found her soft voice and the twinkle in her eyes to be the most potent points of interest. He found himself avoiding parties and his usual gang of dilettantes in favor of seeking out Fanny's company. He spent many hours courting the young woman properly. His friends all looked on in surprise, for none of them could have conceived of Peter giving up the high life, but he did.

Peter and Fanny took long walks on campus and often found themselves sitting on the rocks on the top of a hill called Piney Prospect. The area was secluded and afforded the young couple a certain amount of privacy. As all young lovers do, Fanny and Peter shared many intimate moments.

Unfortunately for Peter, there was another young man at the university who had enjoyed Fanny's affections before Peter had entered the picture. This young man was also from a good family. He felt that Peter had alienated Fanny's affections, and he sought to win her back by challenging Peter to a duel.

Peter was furious when he was challenged. The thought of his Fanny with another man was enough to make his blood boil, and he foolishly accepted the challenge. It was decided that Peter and his rival would meet at Piney Prospect one hot summer's evening. They each asked a friend to be a second for them, and the four young men met secretly.

The duelists paced off at the distance they agreed upon, raised their guns, and at the signal turned to shoot. Peter's bullet went wide, and a second later, he crumpled to the ground mortally wounded. The rival for Fanny's affections rushed to Peter's side along with both seconds. They immediately realized that Peter was soon to depart this life. Ironically, Peter had fallen just beside the rock where he and Fanny enjoyed so many blissful afternoons.

Within moments, Peter was dead. Realizing they were in real trouble, the three men conferred and agreed that Peter's body must be hidden. None of them were willing to give up their lives for this foolish act of bravado that had slain Peter.

One of the men went to fetch shovels, and the other two men levered the rock out of the way. They dug up the earth beneath the rock and quickly rolled Peter into the shallow grave. By now, they were working under the cloak of darkness, but they all felt a need to be free of this spot. They tamped the ground back down and rolled the rock back in place. It was only then that they realized that the rock was covered in Peter's blood. They quickly wiped it clean and hurried away to return the shovels before they were missed.

The next few days were an agony to all involved. The rival for Fanny's affections found that he had won nothing. The poor girl pined for her lost Peter. The school eventually notified Peter's family that he had left, and they attempted to locate him but to no avail. Peter seemed to simply have vanished. The three men who had buried Peter told everyone that he had run off to join the military. No one could prove that they were wrong. In time, however, the story of the duel leaked out. Peter's uncle, Congressman George Dromgoole, came looking for the boy, but he could find out nothing to support the idea that Peter had died in a duel. Later, Peter's roommate wrote a letter, stating that Peter had simply left on his own.

But poor Fanny never stopped longing for her lover. She was unable to make sense of his sudden departure. She was sure that Peter loved her as much as she loved him. His words and deeds had been sincere. It was all a terrible mystery for her. Each day, she walked to Piney Prospect to sit and remember. She sat on the rock where she and Peter had so often cuddled, and she wept for her lost love. She noticed the little red stains in the rock but thought little about them. Little did she know that he was in close proximity.

Eventually, grief claimed Fanny, too. She was buried without ever knowing that her beloved Peter had not left her. For sixty years, the secret of Peter's whereabouts remained a mystery until the shooter confessed on his own deathbed.

There are those who say that Peter and Fanny found happiness on the other side. Legend has it that the couple can be seen sitting on the rock where Peter is supposedly buried. Others claim that either Peter or Fanny alone have been seen still waiting for the other to return. Phantom sobs are heard on occasion, and they are believed to be the sounds of poor Fanny's grief. Folks claim that when it rains the water falling from the rock under which Peter is buried runs red.

It has been said that university personnel have moved the rock to look under it, but Peter's body was not found. The red stains have remained upon the rock to this day, but geologists say that the red is iron ore and not blood. There have been many theories about what happened to Peter Dromgoole. His family speculated that he traveled to Europe; that contention is bolstered by a letter written by Peter just before his disappearance. In the letter, he confided that he was depressed and that he was going to travel. Other family members believe that Peter assumed a new name and joined the army. They claim that he could be traced out west, where years later he died in a shootout.

Perhaps one of the strangest twists in the legend is that the area where Peter was supposedly killed was subsequently purchased by a former student of the University of North Carolina, Edwin Wray Martin, who seemed unusually drawn to the Prospect Hill area. He claimed that it reminded him of a fairy-tale woodland with demons, goblins, and witches. Martin purchased the land and created a sort of fraternity there, which he called The Order of the Gimghouls. He ran the group until his death in 1895. The secret order has remained active and elusive to this very day.

In the early 1920s, the group speculated in land deals in the area and made enough profit to build their own medieval-style castle, which they named Gimghoul Castle. The massive undertaking took four years to complete. There the members meet, hold ceremonies, and carry out secret rituals. It is a very closed-mouthed group and only rarely does a non-member even enter the castle. The secret society, however, printed a version of the Peter Dromgoole legend in a booklet they produced in 1978. The booklet claims that a dark figure appears on the anniversary of Peter's death and points his arm out at Peter's specter, who only arises at the witching hour. The dark figure is the duelist who shot Peter. His spirit cannot rest, because of the unavenged murder he committed. Today, the area of Piney Prospect is privately owned, so no one is allowed to visit the spot where the legend began, but at the University of North Carolina, stories of the restless spirits of Peter Dromgoole and his slayer continue on.

Tuckertown's Local Witch

No one in the mill village of Tuckertown remembered when old Ann Blackhand had not been known as the local witch. She was infamous in that area of Montgomery County for her misdeeds. Some witches are known for being helpful and using their magic for healing, but old Ann was different. She was a black witch who enjoyed causing misery and was feared by the citizens of the town. If anything bad happened, old Ann seemed to be lurking nearby and smirking, as if taking pride in her dirty handiwork.

Ann had a particular pick on the local churches, and it was noted that she disliked certain churchgoing families. Suddenly, one by one, each of the families she despised was plagued by marital discord. Affairs were brought to light mysteriously, and couples who had lived in harmony for many years could not agree on anything. Divorces plagued the Tuckertown churches, and it was not lost on folks that old Ann had been seen repeatedly around the homes of each unfortunate family, just before the strife had begun.

Others claimed that she terrorized children and put spells on them. A story circulated through town that she had given a strange fruit to a little boy who had then become terribly ill. When a neighbor asked who had been around the child just prior to his illness, she learned of old Ann's visit. The neighbor suddenly knew what was wrong. She demanded to see the fruit and found it was large and melon-shaped. The woman cast it into the fireplace and uttered a prayer. The strange fruit suddenly turned to powder and went up the chimney in a puff of smoke. Strangely, the little boy jumped up suddenly, announcing he felt better at the same moment.

Old Ann was a force to be reckoned with through the years, and she offered the beleaguered townspeople no mercy. When a farmer offended her in some way, his cattle went dry. When a merchant placed a thumb on the scales while weighing out goods for old Ann, he suddenly took ill with painful cramps and lost business. On and on it went, until one summer evening when the still, thick air was rent by the sound of old Ann screaming in mortal agony in her little house at the edge of town. The screams went on and on as neighbors gathered outside. No one wanted to venture into the house for fear of old Ann's wrath, but the sound the old woman was making was horrible to hear. Surely the old witch must be dying.

At last a group of ladies entered the structure and found old Ann in her bed writhing in agony. She held her chest and sobbed out in pain. As the women entered the room to try and comfort her, a chair skidded across the floor. The women jumped back as the chair blocked the doorway, but they eventually pushed it out of the way and entered. Inside, old Ann screamed and pleaded for help. The ladies did not know what to do, but their sense of Christian charity took over and they tried to make the old woman comfortable.

Suddenly, a black mass seemed to form above old Ann's body as the woman screamed in terror. The mass became a ball that bounced across the floor before rolling out the door. It went down the steps and outside and then it disappeared. Strangely, after that night, old Ann was a reformed woman. Now she was kindly and loving. She no longer shunned churches or took pleasure in misery. It was as if the evil had literally poured out of her into that black mass and left her behind.

Today, Tuckertown is no more. The site of the town was covered over by a man-made lake, but some people still live within the area and tell the tale of the evil witch who became good.

The Drinking Ghost

In the 1920s, a black woman named Millie Crocket and her passel of children set up housekeeping in an abandoned shack in the woods outside of a village at the edge of Badin Lake. The area was desperately poor, as many black communities were at that time. Prejudice had taken its toll on the people.

Millie made her money by entertaining men for a few cents each. The money was never enough, and matters were made worse by Millie's love of alcohol. This was during Prohibition. Every time Millie had any money in her pocket, she headed out to the local saloon. The proprietress of the saloon was a woman named Beulah Bolen, a wise woman who ran the business from her home. Beulah never allowed the alcohol to be seen and had a rule that no one could verbally ask for it. If someone wanted to get into the saloon, they had to go through Beulah.

Many times, old Millie Crocket pounded on the door of Beulah's house in need of a drink. Beulah demanded to know if she had money before she would let her in. People with money had to pound on a tall cabinet that stood between the kitchen and living room area. If one slapped the top of the cabinet three times, it meant that person wanted corn liquor or whiskey. Two slaps meant the person wanted a beer. Beulah never spoke a word about the alcohol, but she quietly fetched it from her kitchen refrigerator. She did not encourage folks to linger once they bought their booze, but for regular customers her house was a second home.

Old Millie Crocket was well known in the area for her loose ways, her trashy house, and her love of alcohol. She was bold as brass about her need for booze. If she was without money to buy it, she begged, borrowed or stole to get it. Sometimes she broke up private gatherings until she was given a portion of alcohol. She blackmailed local moonshiners for booze. She was often a good investment for them, however, for no one paid the old drunk any mind and she often heard important information that she passed on to the moonshiners who were her pipeline.

As the years went by, her children grew up and eventually left the home. Millie continued to live in the old shack alone. She never maintained the old place, so it moaned and sighed with every storm. Folks thought that they would find Millie crushed to death after every bad storm, but Millie and the shack lingered on.

Millie grew arthritic and crippled, and when she could no longer walk the mountains to find the moonshine stills, she applied for welfare. The checks took the place of the men in her life. She was too old for them to want her, so now the money from the government paid for her booze. Through it all, Beulah Bolen looked down on the old drunkard, but she never refused the old girl's money.

One night, Millie stumbled into Beulah's place and showed Beulah enough money for some beer. Millie was already drunk, but Beulah gave her a beer and sent her on her way. "Go home and sleep," she advised Millie.

When Millie pulled open the front door to leave, a blast of bitter winter air blew in and Beulah shivered. "Goose walked on a grave," she muttered to a customer. The next day Beulah was not surprised to hear that old Millie Crocket had collapsed along the road leading back to her shack. She had died still holding her last precious beer in her hands. The poor old drunk had frozen to death.

Folks buried Millie without much fanfare. Even some of her children did not attend her funeral. The cold winter's day was too bitter for anyone to linger, and so no one even offered a pretense of sympathy. No flowers or music accompanied old Millie.

Time marched on and Millie was all but forgotten except when her name was resurrected as part of a funny story. She became a full-fledged legend in those parts for her many brazen attempts to get alcohol.

Beulah Bolen finally sold beer to the wrong person and she was raided. She spent some time in jail and came back to her community a changed woman. In prison, she got religion. When she returned home she joined the local church, renounced her former ways, and destroyed all of her hidden booze. She lived well enough on her government checks and her savings.

A new minister came to town who caught Beulah's eye. He was an older man, but soon he and Beulah were seen together quite frequently, always in polite company. Rumors circulated that the reformed barkeep and the preacher were going to get married, and the two soon made their engagement official.

Beulah had nearly forgotten old Millie Crocket, who had died nearly two years ago on a cold winter's night. It was winter again and the wind picked at the eves of Beulah's snug little house as she bundled herself into bed. She fell asleep in her chilled bedroom with visions of her impending wedding filling her head.

Suddenly something woke her up. She lay in the darkness waiting and listening. Someone was pounding on her door the way old Millie once had. Beulah heaved a sigh and sat up, plunging her feet into warm slippers. Some old drunken fool had forgotten that she was a reformed woman and had come for beer. She would soon send him packing, she thought with determination as she tightened the sash of her robe.

Downstairs, Beulah looked out the glass top of the door but saw no one. Still the pounding continued. Her memory now brought Millie to mind. She thought of her desperate pounding when her cravings overtook her.

"Nonsense," Beulah muttered, but a small thread of fear crept through her. "Impossible," she whispered aloud, yet she found herself unable to return to her bedroom. Instead she stoked up the fire in her living room and sat down in a chair to watch the door.

As the church bells rang out midnight, the pounding stopped and Beulah froze once more. In her rowdy days, she closed her establishment at midnight. Millie had often gone away at that time to bemoan her fate.

The next day, Beulah almost convinced herself that it had all been her imagination, but later that night, the pounding awoke her with a start. Again, Beulah made her way downstairs and faced the empty porch. Again, she waited in a chair until the church bell tolled and the pounding stopped.

Beulah confided her visitations to the preacher and some of her close friends. She asked them to come and keep a vigil with her. By now, she was convinced that it was the ghost of old Millie coming back from the grave to beg for beer.

The group sat up into the night and waited. To their shock, the pounding on the door began precisely as Beulah had described it. The minister and a couple of the men bundled up and went outside by way of the back door to sneak up on the practical joker who was frightening Beulah. They found that no one was on the porch, even though someone was clearly pounding upon the door. At midnight, the church bells again rang away the invisible spirit.

Before the group departed, someone suggested that Beulah offer the ghost a beer the next night. If it was old Millie, surely she would take it. If not, then they would know that someone else was haunting Beulah. Reluctantly, Beulah accepted the beer with her minister's blessings.

The following night, a larger crowd of friends pushed their way into Beulah's living room to keep the vigil. The wind beat against the windows and made the group glad for the warmth of the old woodstove. Suddenly, the pounding began. Beulah bolstered her courage and flung the door open as she had agreed to do. She cried out, "Millie Crocket, if that's you, come on in and fetch the beer on the yonder cabinet."

With those words Beulah stepped back and shut the door. Everyone waited as their eyes watched the beer can on the old cabinet from which Beulah formerly served her customers. The can quivered and suddenly rose up. Then it tipped itself over and the beer poured into an invisible something or someone. As soon as the can was empty, it was slapped back down on the cabinet.

The clink of the can hitting the wooden cabinet top seemed to break the spell and everyone suddenly began to run for the door.

Coats, hats, and boots were grabbed in the mad dash to get away from the ghost. Folks ran for the comfort of their homes and poor old Beulah had to hobble along to a friend's home to find a decent night's sleep.

Beulah soon moved out of the house, and the memories of her former life seemed to quell the romance she had so enjoyed. But Beulah was not the only person old Millie sought out for visits. Soon word spread all over town that Millie's spirit was back, and it was more thirsty for brew than the woman had ever been during her life. Folks found their doors swept open by an invisible force that threw open the refrigerator door and stole beer. Many a person stood in stupefied amazement as they watched the beer pour down an invisible gullet. Then Millie dropped the can and seemed to be gone. The old moonshiners watched jugs of good corn liquor drained instantly. Everyone in town became terrified of the drunken old ghost.

As the years passed, old Millie seemed to settle down. Her raids became less frequent. But every now and then, at a community gathering, an elder will open a can of brew and sit it at an empty place. It is an offering for the drunken ghost, so that she will leave everyone alone while they have a good time without fear that their beer will be stolen by the drinking ghost.

Ghost Steps at the White-Holman House

Raleigh is a beautiful city filled with grand houses. The White-Holman House, built in the Georgian-Federal transition style, is one of the oldest mansions in the city. The history of this grand structure is shrouded in mystery, for no one seems completely sure of when the house was built or by whom. The most accurate guess is that it was built around 1799 for William White, who was the North Carolina secretary of state from 1798 until 1810. The house was part of the White estate when it was acquired by William C. Holman of Massachusetts in December 1884. Holman and his wife, Anna, raised their four daughters in the house. The four ladies later inherited the house and lived there together in their later years. During the family's tenure, William Holman made a large number of improvements and renovations to the house. He had an entire wing of the mansion removed from the structure, which was later used in an entirely new house nearby. He had a back staircase walled up, because the family did not use it. The staircase, however, still exists behind the wall. It seems that someone from the distant past is still using the stairs. Throughout the years, many people have reported hearing the distinctive thump-step of a person with a peg leg going up and down that staircase in the wall. Who the figure might be is a mystery. For those who have heard the tread, however, there is little doubt that someone is walking up and down the secret stairs.

Speculation has run rampant through the years as to the identity of the unknown peg-legged ghost. Some have suggested that it must be a servant, as no known resident of the house ever lost a leg. Others claim that it is a visiting spirit who stayed on in the house for his own reasons. Yet another theory says it is a slave who lost his leg in some mishap and is still loyally toiling in his master's home.

Despite the lack of identity, this ghostly traveler continues his relentless thud-thumping in the walls of the stately mansion.

Lydia's Last Ride

They call them phantom hitchhikers, and their stories are categorized as urban legends. But every so often a ghostly tale of a traveling spirit touches the public consciousness. It has been this way for a young woman known in the Greensboro area as Lydia.

On U.S. Highway 70, there is an underpass that has a strange history. Since 1923, folks have reported seeing a young woman in a long, white party dress, hitchhiking for a ride. The pretty girl has stopped many motorists through the years. She always gets into the car and asks the driver to take her to an address in the nearby High Point area. She chats amiably, telling the driver that she was at a dance in Raleigh that evening and was on her way home when she had car trouble. She says that she left her car and began to walk toward home and that she fears her mother will be terribly worried about her.

The driver usually listens politely and assures the girl that she will be home soon. The girl falls silent at this point, as if terribly worried. She clasps her hands anxiously and watches the road ahead.

When the car nears the address in High Point, the driver turns to the girl, only to find she has vanished.

Some drivers are so shocked that they just drive on and never stop at the address. Those who do stop and knock on the door of the house find themselves listening to a strange tale. The person who lives at the house says that they are aware of the girl named Lydia and that her story is true. She had been at a party in Raleigh and was returning home when her car broke down. The girl had been struck by another vehicle as she stood along the road waiting for help. They tell the driver that Lydia is still trying to go home, but she never makes it.

The Haunted State Capitol

North Carolina's State Capitol was built of massive squares of granite cut from the earth. It is a large and imposing structure which has seen a great deal of history. Built in 1840, it was standing at the time of the Civil War. The building is three stories high, with the first floor housing the governor's office in one wing and staff offices in the rest of the space. The second floor also includes offices, as well as the original Senate and House chambers, now open to the public. Though no longer used by the General Assembly (who have been meeting since 1963 in the North Carolina State Legislative Building), the chambers have been pressed into service within the last few years for various ceremonial purposes. On the third floor is the State Library, geologist's office, and two galleries that look down on the chambers.

Through the years, the Capitol has earned a reputation for its beauty . . . and its ghosts.

Raymond Beck has made the history of North Carolina and the State Capitol his life's work. He was the Capitol Curator for many years. When Ray first heard the ghost stories, he dismissed them as folklore, but in 1981, he had an experience that changed his mind.

It was a soft spring night and Ray was working in the library. It was getting late, but Ray was deep into his work. He walked over to the shelves to replace some books, when the strangest feeling suddenly consumed him. He suddenly felt with absolute certainly that he was no longer alone in the room. Ray looked around but saw nothing. He shrugged off the feeling and went back to work, trying to ignore the sensation. Then it dissipated.

Ray had just about convinced himself that it had been his imagination, when the overwhelming presence returned. This time it was even stronger and Ray looked about quickly. As he expected, he saw nothing, but then he began to consider the old ghost stories in a new light. Perhaps they really were true.

For some time, Ray kept his story to himself, but then he decided to tell it to the Capitol administrator, Sam Townsend Sr., whom he considered a good friend as well as his boss. Sam spent many years at the Capitol dealing with the pragmatic concerns of his work. As an engineer, he was always a practical man, but on that day Sam surprised Ray by saying that something strange had happened to him in the building. Ray listened with great interest as Sam described almost exactly the same experience.

It was about 8 P.M. on an early summer evening in 1976 when Sam was sitting at a desk in the governor's office doing paperwork. The Capitol had been renovated but not yet been reopened. Sam gradually began to notice the sound of keys rattling in the lock at the north entrance, directly across the building from where he sat. He paid scant attention to the keys at first, because he assumed that Thad Eure, the secretary of state, was coming in to work for a while, too. He clearly heard the heavy door opening and the sound of footsteps crossing the floor on the other side of the building. Sam stood up and walked to Eure's office, but found no one was there. He would have sworn he had heard the heavy door open only seconds earlier.

While he stood there, he heard the keys rattle again, but this time they were at the south door. Sam paused and waited, but no one entered. He initiated a search of the building, but no one was found. Months later, Sam had another unexplainable experience. His office had been moved to the second floor into the area where the clerk of the Senate had once had an office. This was in the northeast side of the chamber. On that evening, Sam was again working late. Again he heard footsteps. The steps seemed to be coming from the old committee room where Ray Beck now worked. Sam waited until the footsteps were close and then opened the door, expecting to talk to Ray. To his surprise the hall was empty. From that point on, Sam heard the phantom footsteps each night at approximately the same time. No matter how many times he looked, he never saw anyone in the hall. Strangely, the steps stopped when a copy machine was moved into the area.

Sam had one more unexplained series of experiences in the Capitol. One night, he was walking toward the Senate chamber when he saw someone standing in the doorway. For just a second he caught a glimpse of a figure before it vanished. On another night, he actually had to sidestep a gray figure in the rotunda. The specter floated past, paying no attention at all to the very surprised Sam. The idea of ghosts never sat well with Sam, but he never was able to find a rational explanation for his experiences.

Owen Jackson worked in the Capitol as a guard. He was there alone at night until his shift ended at half past midnight. The older gentleman spent more than twelve years making his nightly rounds through the building. Many times through the years, Owen heard sounds that he was unable to explain. He had his first experience on the first week he worked there—he heard a woman singing "Nearer My God to Thee" over and over. Owen thought a radio or tape was left playing, so he hunted through the building to find the source; he found nothing. He was more than a little unnerved, for the voice kept repeating the song. When Owen's shift was over, he called the Capitol Police to report it. The dispatcher replied, "You won't catch me up there!"

Perhaps one of the most common things Owen dealt with was the sound of falling books from the shelves of the State Library. Invariably, Owen would check the library, only to find the books neatly tucked away on the shelves. He never found any rational explanation for the sound. For Owen, though, it was just another in a long line of mysterious noises he heard at the Capitol. He heard phantom keys jingling down hallways, footsteps where no one was treading, and on at least one occasion, a glass window breaking. Each noise was duly checked out, but there was never any explanation for the sounds. Owen would just continue his work, trusting that the spirits were kind souls who would not hurt him.

Only once was Owen frightened by a sound. It was a dark, stormy night, and Owen listened as the storm spent its fury. About midnight, Owen made his rounds and returned to the front reception desk. He had just sat down when the long, terrifying scream of a woman shattered the night. It seemed to be coming from the floor above him. Owen jumped out of his seat and looked up the stairs. He froze there and waited. He said he waited because, he thought, "If she really needs me, she'll scream again." But there were no further screams, so Owen just went on with his work as if all were normal.

Owen experienced more than just sounds though. One night, as he was about to do his rounds, he began to stand up from his chair when he felt a hand push him by the shoulder back down into his seat. He felt there was a reason for this, so he did not resist and waited until the hand on his shoulder went away before getting up again.

Then there was the elevator. It had a tendency to operate on its own. Often Owen saw the elevator light up suddenly, indicating its movement from floor to floor. The doors sometimes opened up as if someone was using it, but he never saw anyone. Owen himself never used it. He had no intention of being stuck in an elevator with a ghost.

Owen's station was at a reception desk in the east hall, facing the elevator and men's restroom. Late one night, Owen was surprised when a small woman wearing a blue choir robe with white piping opened the men's room door and stepped out. She then walked right through the glass of the locked front doors and simply faded away.

Owen saw a figure one cold, clear night on the second floor. He had hurried outside to start his car to warm it up when he glanced up at the building. Through a second-floor window, he saw a glowing figure move past. The window shade was partly drawn, but he was able to make out a gray uniform, such as one a Confederate soldier had worn. Owen said he could actually see the buttons on the uniform shining in the light. Owen knew, however, that no one was in the building, so he slipped the car into gear and went home.

A retired maintenance staff member, a Mr. Johnson, also reported many strange experiences. He heard voices, saw shadowy figures, and felt a presence in the building on several occasions. One experience, however, was unique and noteworthy. Johnson was working on the second floor of the building early one morning before the staff arrived. He was vacuuming and dusting the desks in the chambers when a motion from the gallery above caught his eye. He looked up and was shocked to see a fellow employee watching him work.

He was shocked, because this person, a friend with whom he had cleaned the building for years, had died months earlier.

These paranormal experiences are not limited to the staff of the Capitol. In the 1980s, Jane Barbot was on the board of the nonprofit State Capitol Foundation. One of the duties of the organization was to decorate the building for Christmas. Jane was with her husband and a friend, Ernie Fuller, working late into the night. At 1:30 A.M., they were putting up Christmas trees in the rotunda niches. They finished one niche and moved on to the next one, when they realized that the tree in the northwestern niche had nearly fallen over. They adjusted it and moved on. Throughout the night, the tree in that niche kept falling, no matter how they tried to secure it.

The following day, the decorating committee was called by the staff to say that the tree had slipped yet again. Ernie returned the next evening to stabilize the tree with a piece of plywood. As he worked, he suddenly felt a hand upon his shoulder. For a moment he froze, but he knew that no one was in the area with him. Rather than panic, however, he felt a sense of peace wash over him. He simply finished his work and left, but he knew that a spirit had been with him in the building.

Jane related that her husband was also pushed in the building one evening while he was alone. It was a gentle push and he was not upset by the experience.

In 2001, Rhine Research Center contracted to have paranormal investigators research the State Capitol. Along with their own psychic investigator, Anne Poole, they authorized the Ghost Research Foundation (GRF) of Pennsylvania to carry out the research. The team set up equipment, monitored the area, and worked with the help of the staff at the Capitol, including Raymond Beck. When the team leader first sat down to do an in-depth interview with Beck, she noticed a flash of movement. As she glanced to the side, she saw a young man with dark hair in clothing from the Civil War era laughing at her. The young man seemed amused by the interview. He stayed there for almost a minute but disappeared when she glanced away to get Beck's attention. When she confided this to Beck and showed him the seat, he confirmed that others had seen a spirit in that seat as well.

The investigations of the facility with GRF through the years garnered some interesting results. The team worked there one weekend a year through 2006, and in that time they recorded what they believe to be phantom voices and a ghostly mass on the security cameras.

Perhaps one of the most interesting experiences occurred during their last visit in 2006. Beck and Scott Crownover of the GRF were in the central rotunda speaking with some guests, when the investigators throughout the building began hurrying toward them and demanding to know what had happened. Was someone hurt? Had they fallen down the stairs? The folks in the rotunda were puzzled. They had heard nothing, but could tell from the frightened looks upon the faces of the rest of the team that something had happened. Everyone in the building, except for those actually in the center of the rotunda, heard what sounded like the scream of someone falling down the stairs. Despite the fact that people were spread out over three floors and in different wings of the structure, they all darted to the same spot after hearing the scream. The puzzle of how everyone in the building heard the screams except those in the area where it seemed to originate was never solved. On two different levels of the building and in different wings, however, investigators were attempting to record electronic voice phenomena (EVP). According to the investigators, both tape recorders clearly caught the loud scream.

Are spirits wandering the North Carolina State Capitol? The array of sightings and the caliber of those reporting the events lend great credence to this most unique and beautiful building's haunted history.

Governor Fowle's Bed

Daniel Gould Fowle was the first governor of North Carolina to live in the Executive Mansion in Raleigh that was completed in early 1891. He is remembered not only for his tenure in the building, but also for a heavy bed that he designed. The governor gave specifications to his workmen for a heavy, ornate bed, which he slept in throughout the rest of his time in office, which was brief. He, in fact, died in the bed shortly after moving into the mansion that same year.

Through the years, the bed stayed in place and became a fixture in the beautiful mansion. Perhaps the huge old wooden bed remained in the house because of its comfort or style or simply because it had become a tradition—every governor thereafter to 1970 slept in the bed, until Bob Scott broke the run.

Governor Scott did not like the bed and ordered it removed from the executive bedroom. He had it placed in another bedroom on the third floor that was rarely used and out of his sight. Governor Scott had very particular tastes and wanted something more modern. It seemed like a simple thing really, but Governor Scott was about to find out that he was not only bucking tradition, he was offending the very indignant spirit of Governor Fowle.

Almost as soon as the bed was moved to the inconspicuous bedroom, trouble began. At night, there was pounding within the wall where the headboard of Governor Fowle's bed once stood. Scott and his family quickly realized that something was wrong. Each night at about 10 P.M. the thudding began. As the hour grew later, the sounds grew more intense until finally dying down very late at night. The thumping and pounding in the wall continued on throughout Scott's term. By the time he left office, his family and staff had attributed the noise to Governor Fowle. Scott refused to bow to the ghost's demands, taking the whole thing in stride. He seemed to find the noisy spirit amusing.

The next governor requested that Fowle's bed be placed back in the Executive Bedroom, although he never revealed why he did so. It is said with the return of his beloved bed, Governor Fowle seemed satisfied and allowed the new governor to rest peacefully. No governor since Scott has been bold enough to move the bed again. Since the bed's return, there have been no more stories about hauntings in the Executive Mansion.

The White Horse of Poole's Woods

William Poole was a man before his time. He saw the world in a different way than most of his affluent counterparts of the mid-nineteenth century. He was a man who had worked his way up in life. It is said that he started his fortune with a mere fifty cents, but from that tiny acorn grew mighty oaks, literally, for William Poole was a conservationist. He owned more than sixteen hundred acres of land, most of it densely wooded. He rose to wealth before the Civil War and had a fine home, luxuries, and many slaves. He would scarcely have been called frugal, except when it came to trees.

William Poole loved trees. He loved watching them grow. He enjoyed partaking of their shade. A large part of his acreage was devoted to growing trees.

Poole spent a great deal of time riding through the wilderness he nurtured. Every day, he mounted his favorite horse, a beautiful white stallion. On their rides, the horse seemed to anticipate Poole's needs. If Poole wanted to stop and linger in an area, the horse was content to do so. If Poole felt the urge for speed, the massive horse carried him rapidly toward their destination.

Poole was a large, handsome, sturdy man, who was friendly and outgoing. For some time, he courted a young woman from a good family in Johnston County. She was considered one of the most beautiful women in the area, and many of the locals thought Poole and the girl would make a fine match. But sadly, Poole and the young woman parted ways. After this broken love affair, William Poole would never marry.

Poole retreated to his forest, marking trees to cut and keeping an eye on every part of his own private acreage. He was a happy man until the Union Army invaded the South. Poole listened and watched along with everyone else as the hated Union forces inched ever closer to his home. An astute businessman, Poole attempted to liquidate his assets and hide his valuables deep in the woods where he felt they might be safe.

The most valuable thing he had, aside from his woods, was his beautiful white horse. Poole kept the horse with him as long as possible, but he knew that when the Union forces arrived every available animal would be conscripted, and he could not bear to think of a damnable Yankee riding his beloved horse into battle. He knew that he would have to hide the horse and his fortune well or the Yankees would have both.

When Raleigh fell to Union forces, Poole knew that he must hide all of his possessions that he wished to keep. Union general William T. Sherman believed that by breaking the will of the people, he could bring the war to a close. His army was literally burning its way across the South. Anything that could not be carried away was destroyed. Poole realized that his home and most of his possessions must be forfeited, and he accepted that fate, but there were certain things that he would protect and save.

When the Union forces reached Raleigh, they sought out the wealthy families there to plunder. Although Sherman gave general orders not to loot Raleigh, a bit of thievery among the officers was ignored. Soon Union troops showed up at Poole's home. He greeted them stoically and pretended to be friendly. The officers were fairly direct. They had heard that Poole had a fortune in gold buried around the property and they wanted it. He sat on his front porch and shook his head. It is true that he had had gold, but the fortune had been much exaggerated by local folks, he said. He lost a good portion of it during the war and some had been stolen, too. He now had his home and little else. The Union forces did not believe him. Their intelligence said that there was gold and some very good horse flesh on that estate and they meant to find it.

The soldiers tied Poole to a rail and dragged him down to his corn cribs. He was injured but still refused to talk. They began burning buildings, but still Poole was stoic.

Soldiers scattered on horseback to search for the gold. Deep in the forest, they heard a horse whinnying. The men followed the sound and found the white horse tied in a little grove, where they might never have looked had the horse not called out. The soldiers were well pleased with the fine horse and took it with them.

The Union soldiers found no gold but a Union officer rode away on the back of the white stallion. The horse fought to throw the strange rider, but the officer held the mount and Poole never saw his beloved companion again.

Poole survived, but those who knew him said that he lost heart after his horse was stolen. He grieved for it as a man would for a person. He died in 1889 at the age of ninety-three, after living a very productive life. He had been a businessman, justice, and county commissioner. When he died, he left instructions in his will to protect the woods. He wrote: "until the division of my land hereinafter provided for shall be made, 75 acres on the west side of this tract shall be preserved in original growth as it stands now without a single tree being cut or hauled from it."

It took years to sort out Poole's will, and during that time local folks began to talk. They said that at night they saw Poole astride the white stallion riding through his forests as he had done in life. Others saw the spirit of the horse running free, as if trying to return to Poole. Still others heard phantom footsteps and claimed that Poole was still watching over the property.

In time, the will did get sorted out, and parcels of the land were sold off for homes. Today, Poole's Woods is part of a housing development, but there are those who claim that the old man and his horse still ride free.

The Devil's Tramping Ground

Europeans first settled in North Carolina more than three hundred years ago. Ten miles west of the area that is known today as Siler City, those settlers found a strange formation in a forest that puzzled them—a forty-foot circle in which nothing would grow. The area appeared to be tramped down, but no one could find a reasonable explanation for it. At first the settlers thought the ring was where the natives performed rituals, but in time they found that the natives avoided the spot.

Through the years, people have come up with some creative stories to explain the circle, but the one story that stuck was that of the Devil's visit there. As he was thinking how to spread evil, he paced round and round. All night he walked around until he had carved out the strange, vegetation-free ring in the wilderness of Chatham County, now known as the Devil's Tramping Ground.

But vegetation is not the only thing that is compelled to stay away. It is said that the Devil throws out anything—or anyone—that lands in his circle. There are many stories of people placing objects in it only to find them moved moments later. Occasionally, people have tried to spend the night inside the circle. Either they grew so uncomfortable that they had to leave the ring or else they awake to find themselves and their camping gear outside of it.

It was said that bad luck would follow anyone who dared to take a souvenir from the Devil's Tramping Ground. There are stories of folks who took rocks or small stones, only to bring them back after experiencing a series of increasingly bad events. Some people today believe that the circle was actually from a UFO landing in the area. It is suggested that the craft burned away the grass and possibly soaked the ground with radiation, thus causing the void.

Through the years, scientists have studied the area to solve the mystery. The ground was tested and found to have an extraordinarily high salt content. How the salt got there is open to debate.

The Devil's Tramping Ground is on County Road 1100, approximately two miles from Harper's Crossroads. Go see it and draw your own conclusion!

The Ghostly Gang of Hannah's Creek Swamp

The Civil War inspired great acts of bravery, but it was also a catalyst for depravity. Throughout the war, civilians of the South were targeted by bands of marauders who rode in to steal whatever was left of value after the Union soldiers had passed through. These marauders became especially prevalent at the end of the war after Sherman's March.

Confederate lieutenant John Saunders was devastated when he got word that his parents' home near Smithfield had been raided by marauders. The band of outlaws had taken everything of value, murdered his mother and his father, and burned the house down. There was nothing Saunders could do, however, for he was duty-bound to stay with his men.

Weeks later, Saunders heard that there was a group of raiders living near Hannah's Creek Swamp. He and his men began to make contact with the group in order to draw them out. Saunders and his men rode into the area late one evening, ostensibly to purchase goods, but they meant to arrest the thieving band for their crimes.

The leader of the marauders was David Fanning. The mob he led consisted of more than fifty men. Fanning was a cunning man who chose as a base of operations an island in Hannah's Creek Swamp, because it was a desolate place and they had virtual control of it. For Fanning, the war was an opportunity to get rich. He was loyal to the Union Army, and so officials turned a blind eye to his activities. Fanning cared nothing for the loss and pain he left in his wake.

The marauders were quickly subdued and Fanning was apprehended. Saunders watched as his men unearthed the loot and tossed the items into a pile. The lieutenant became furious thinking

about how items such as wedding rings and necklaces had been confiscated. One item, taken from Fanning himself, caught the lieutenant by surprise. It was a gold cross. Saunders examined it closely. With trembling fingers, he caressed the crucifix. He had held this same crucifix in his hands many times as a child; it had belonged to his mother. With blazing eyes, he looked at Fanning and demanded to know where the cross came from, but he did not need the answer. The crucifix was proof that this was the gang of murderers who had killed his parents. A white fury shook Saunders. He turned suddenly and ordered that Fanning's men be hanged immediately—all except for Fanning.

The murderers were not so brave when it was their turn to die, and many of them begged for their lives. Fanning, too, pleaded to be spared. It fell on deaf ears, and Saunders proceeded with the executions, hanging all the men but Fanning. When the lieutenant and his men rode away with their sole prisoner, a grisly sight was left behind. More than fifty corpses were swinging in the trees as the wind wafted mist around them.

Saunders then led his men toward his burned-out home at Smithfield. When they arrived, Saunders took Fanning to the family cemetery, where he personally hanged him in view of his parents' graves.

Through the years, people who have braved visiting Hannah's Creek Swamp have come back with strange tales to tell. They claim that voices come from the trees in the swamp. The voices can be heard begging for their lives. They say the loudest of all is that of David Fanning.

A Presence at Mill Creek Bridge

Old Squire had been a slave in the home of a Mr. Lynch for many years. He had been sold on the block more than once and seen great sorrow in his time, but his tenure with Lynch had been both his longest and most difficult. Lynch was not an agreeable or pleasant man. It was a cross that Old Squire had to bear.

Old Squire had converted to Christianity long ago and preached a bit on Sundays down in the slave quarters. Even some of the white folks treated him with respect. Lynch, however, razzed the old man constantly, finding fault with everything he did.

Lynch was in a particularly foul mood one day in 1820. He pulled Old Squire out of the gardens to send him down to Mill Creek Bridge, where he said he needed work done. Old Squire hobbled along to keep up, but Lynch felt no concern that Old Squire suffered from painful arthritis most of the time.

At the Mill Creek Bridge, Lynch showed Old Squire a spot where the stones were coming loose and insisted that the bridge immediately needed repaired. Sitting down, Lynch berated the old man, who began to painfully pick up the stones to put them back in place. Lynch, who was carrying a walking stick, got up and struck Old Squire several times with it to get his attention about some detail that failed to suit his notions of how the work should be done. As Lynch shouted, Old Squire grew angrier and angrier. Then Lynch brought the stick down over the old man's arthritic hands, and Old Squire cried out painfully.

"Get up and do your work," Lynch snarled, "And this time do it right."

As Old Squire held his hands and glared at the hateful man, something seemed to take possession of him. He reached out and snatched the stick away from a very surprised Lynch, who looked at Old Squire in shock before the old man brought the stick down on Lynch's head. Within seconds, a lifetime of pent-up anger was released and Lynch lay dead.

Old Squire knew that he had to hurry. He hid the body in the stone abutment and finished piling rocks up on it. He threw the bloody stick away and ran home as fast as he could. When he got there, he gathered up what food he had and disappeared.

When Lynch did not return home, word was sent out that he was missing. Folks were so busy looking for the rich man that they failed to notice that the old slave was also gone. At first, folks believed that whatever fate befell Lynch had also befallen Old Squire, but eventually, Lynch's body was found and the law set out after Old Squire. The old man had several days head start, though, and he was never found.

It is said that Lynch haunted Mill Creek Bridge for many years. He was never seen, but an unknown presence filled passersby with anger and fear. The presence grabbed objects from travelers' hands, and more than one person ran away in horror from the unseen entity that haunted the bridge. It was a most hateful spirit to encounter.

Western Piedmont

THE WESTERN PIEDMONT IS CHARACTERIZED BY A MORE GENTLE ghostlore. Here ghosts move quietly through the night, seeking to warn the living that all may not be well in the spirit world. The spirits here are helpful and sometimes loving. Who would not be touched by the spirit who haunts Brothers House? The Western Piedmont is also home to a variety of strange creatures and monsters. The Santer Cat wanders these parts and a sea monster lives in a man-made lake in the area.

The Wreck at Bostian Bridge

It was a warm morning on August 27, 1891, in Salisbury. Passengers boarding the 1:30 A.M. train headed to Asheville were tired and listless. They wanted nothing more than to settle in their seats and rest. Most of the passengers fell asleep to the hiss of steam and the clackety-clack of the train moving down the tracks.

At 3:00 A.M., passengers were awakened by a violent rocking as the train bucked sideways. Those who were near windows looked out and saw that the train was crossing the Bostian Bridge, a stone structure near the town of Statesville. Suddenly, there was a loud rasp of metal. Passengers screamed as the first car derailed and tipped beyond gravity's ability to push it back on the tracks. The rest of the cars fell like dominoes into the water.

Within seconds, water flooded the darkened cars. The hiss of steam, the sounds of metal twisting, and the screams of the injured broke the stillness of the night.

It it took a while before railroad workers realized that the train had not reached its next stop on time. In the meantime, men, women, and children fought to help each other out of the creek and stabilize the injured. In all, twenty-two people died at Bostian Bridge that night. It was the worst train wreck in North Carolina's history.

For fifty years, there were no ghost stories about Bostian Bridge. But then on the anniversary of the crash, a woman's car broke down near Bostian Bridge at 3:00 A.M. As she waited for daylight and help to arrive, the woman was startled to see the light of a train moving through the darkness. The roaring sound, and then the train's whistle, pierced the night's silence. As the woman stood back watching the train go by, it suddenly swayed and she could hear the terrible sound of screeching metal as the train left the track. The woman was terrified as she saw the train derail and heard the first screams from the passengers. She saw people moving as the train fell more than sixty feet into the water. The woman's feet seemed to move of their own accord and she rushed forward, sliding down the embankment to help the injured. Water splashed her and she cried out that she was going to get help.

With those words, the woman turned and climbed back up the embankment to flag down a car. Someone pulled over, and she breathed a sigh of relief when she saw it was her husband, who had been out looking for her.

Frantically, the woman pulled her husband from the car and pushed him toward the bridge. She gasped out her story, but then she stopped dead. There was nothing in the water. The train, the people—it was all gone.

Later, the couple did some research on the bridge and was shocked to find out that the woman had witnessed the wreck fifty years after the crash.

The Brown Mountain Lights

Most of Brown Mountain Ridge is part of the Pisgah National Forest. It is here that mysterious lights have been observed for hundreds of years. The best place to see the lights is from Wiseman's View, near Morgantown in Burke County.

The Brown Mountain Lights, as they are called, appear after darkness falls. On any given night, cars will park along Route 105 to watch the spectacle. A red light the size of a soccer ball becomes visible and floats above the ground before winking out. Then a light will appear in a different place and the process will repeat itself over and over. One of the oddities of the light is that not everyone will see it the same way. Some see a different colored light or it moves differently for them. But no one denies that strange lights dance in the night air on Brown Mountain.

The most popular accounts of the lights appeared in 1850, when a woman went missing from a mountain community. For days, locals searched for her. Suspicion soon fell on her husband, as people began to whisper that he had done away with her and hid the body somewhere. One night, the searchers noticed a light up on the mountain and wondered if someone was up there. They searched but found no one. The following night the lights appeared again. They continued to be seen the next night and the one after that. Now people wondered if there was a correlation between the missing woman and the mysterious lights. Was she perhaps signaling up on the mountain to tell them where she was?

During the initial investigation, no evidence was found of the woman or her whereabouts. Although folks were suspicious of the husband, there was no evidence against him. Talk turned back to the story of the missing woman when it was discovered that her husband had also gone missing. Eventually the lights disappeared from the mountain and for a time folks forgot about the story.

Years went by before the old story was recalled. Someone walking on the mountain found the skeletal remains of a murdered woman. Some locals remembered the old story of the missing woman and said that she had been found at last. Strangely, when her body was removed from the mountain, the lights returned again. From that time, according to the story, the lights on Brown Mountain have appeared almost nightly.

Historically speaking, however, there have been stories of the lights appearing for hundreds of years, even before the first European settlement. The Catawba and Cherokee Indians saw the lights and had their own legends to explain them. There is a legend that dates back approximately eight hundred years that says that the lights were the spirits of brave warriors who watched over the mountain.

Explanations for the lights run from swamp gas to phosphorus or radium rays created by some means on the mountain. In 1771, German engineer Geraud de Brahm saw the lights and wrote his observations down in his journal: "The mountains emit nitrous vapors which are borne by the wind and when laden winds meet each other the niter inflames." The federal government sent two geological surveys to the area to look into the cause of the lights. The first survey was sent out in 1916, but they added little to the study. In 1922, a second survey team was sent to the area, lead by scientist George Rogers Mansfield. He insisted that the lights were caused by multiple sources. Among them were brush fires, seismic disturbances, and even fireflies. Whatever the explanation for the lights, Brown Mountain is home to an enduring mystery that fascinates all who experience it.

Lake Norman's Monster

Lake Norman is a man-made lake on the Catawba River, which powers nuclear and hydroelectric stations. It was named for former Duke Power president Norman Cocke. The lake has a surface area of more than 32,475 acres. It has 520 miles of shoreline and is larger than the ten other lakes on the Catawba River combined.

For many years, people who enjoy fishing, boating, or hiking at Lake Norman have come away with strange tales of a creature in the lake. It is described as long and gray, brown, or earth-colored, and some say it has an alligator snout. Interestingly, people have been consistently reporting sightings of alligators in Lake Norman and the surrounding lakes for years. The debate about alligators seemed to have ended in 2001, however, when a video was made of an alligator sunning itself on the shores of Lake Wylie, the next lake downstream from Lake Norman. Until that time, no one believed that alligators could survive the winters on the lake or that they had traveled that far inland. It is speculated that the hydroelectric and nuclear power plants warm areas where they pour out water, and the alligators take refuge in those areas in the winter months.

Even stranger is the fact that this man-made lake is home to a rare species of freshwater jellyfish that has never before been found in the Catawba River or its environs. How the jellyfish got there is another mystery.

But how does this tie in with a lake monster? Many folks who have seen the creature argue that something large is in the lake and the existence of the jellyfish and the alligators prove that where there is a habitat, nature will adapt it for its own uses. Some folks have suggested that the monster is really a large alligator, which has mutated to a giant because of its proximity to the nuclear power station. Others speculate that the monster could be a giant snake-head fish, sturgeon, or even a freshwater eel. Currently the idea of a giant snakehead fish is favored since one was caught in Lake Wylie a few years ago.

Reports of the strange Lake Norman creature continue to surface. Consider this quote from the site www.lakenormanmonster.com: "Crusin' along, water skiing, and this huge black thing, about 10 feet long, was whipping along beside me, as fast as I was skiing." And from the same site comes this one: "In the moonlight, I saw two large humps rise above the surface several times. Needless to say, we sped out of there."

Louise

Davidson College was built in 1837 and named for a local Revolutionary War hero, Gen. William L. Davidson. In 1893, the school established the North Carolina Medical College, which offered room and board for a price along with the $75 tuition. The price did not include an important staple needed by medical students—cadavers. Procuring a cadaver was one of the most difficult tasks given to medical students. Some students procured an inexpensive cadaver through a body snatcher.

On the campus at that time, medical students were housed at Chambers Hall, a large, white-columned dormitory. There has long been a legend associated with Chambers Hall that it is haunted by a young woman whom the medical students dubbed Louise.

How Louise came to haunt the building is a fascinating tale. In the most popular version of the story, four medical students went to town by wagon one evening to seek some much-earned entertainment. The young men were drinking quite a bit and during the course of the night they overheard a conversation about the tragic events in one prominent local family. The eavesdropping students learned that a young woman had died only a couple days earlier. The teenage daughter had just been laid to rest and her family was devastated by their loss.

As the young men listened, it struck them that this might be a source for a cadaver. Had they not been inebriated they would have realized that this was a foolish notion. Stealing a body from a prominent family could have far-reaching implications if it was discovered.

The idea of digging up the girl became more appealing as the men continued to drink. Late that night, they went to the local cemetery and located the grave. They found shovels in a shed on the property and quickly dug up the casket. They pried it open and removed the girl, stowing her in the back of the wagon. The men then swiftly reburied the empty casket.

With their prize in back, the men returned to Chambers Hall, where the body was surreptitiously carried up the stairs to be hidden in one of their dorm rooms. The next day, they planned to boil the corpse to remove the flesh from the bones. The school provided a large pot for just that purpose, but early the next morning they were aroused by a terrible rainstorm.

The men did not know it, but that storm would lead to their undoing. The father of the dead girl had gone to the cemetery to grieve and discovered that the rain had washed the thin layer of dirt off the poorly reinterred casket. He had the groundskeeper uncover it and discovered his daughter's body was missing. Immediately, the man came to the conclusion that his daughter's body had been desecrated by someone from the college. It was well-known locally that the students haunted the cemeteries looking for likely corpses to steal.

The father of the girl was infuriated by what had happened. In righteous indignation and horror, he summoned the sheriff, and the two men went to the college. The college president assured the men that his students had nothing to do with stealing the body of the girl, but the paltry assurances and pasty platitudes were not enough to satisfy the enraged father. He demanded that the sheriff make a thorough search for his daughter's body.

The men accompanied the campus officials on the search. One of the most likely spots was Chambers Hall, where the physicians-in-training lived. Room by room the search commenced. The four culprits heard the commotion and roused themselves. When they learned of the search, they flew into a panic. A hurried conference was held in the room where the body was secreted. What should they do? Where should they put the body? If the corpse was found with them, they would be automatically expelled. They had to get rid of it somehow, but how?

They certainly were unable to carry it down the stairs in view of their fellow classmates and the sheriff. It would not be possible to disguise it in such a way for them to remove it from the building. What was left? The attic! There was an unused space at the top of the building where the corpse could be secreted. Even if the body was discovered, no one would be able to prove who had taken it, and that would at least keep them from being expelled.

The men lit a lantern and managed to get the body to the attic. They looked around desperately for some place to hide the corpse, but none came to hand. Then one of the men noticed the tall pillars of the building terminated in the attic and were capped by wooden slabs. The cap on one pillar was slightly loose and they managed to pry it up all the way. They slipped the body down inside the pillar and recapped the top well enough that a cursory look would not reveal an obvious disturbance.

The young men then scattered to their rooms to attempt looking innocent. The culprit who had housed the body overnight noticed a gold locket on the floor of his room and quickly pocketed it. The locket had been worn by the girl, but the chain had apparently been broken in their haste to move the body.

Suddenly, there was a sharp knock on his door. The young medical student opened it to find that the searchers were ready to enter his room. In a fever of fear, the young man watched as they checked all of the obvious places. The father of the dead girl was raving as he watched the search. He was nearly beside himself in pain and anger, and the young medical student suddenly felt remorse for his actions and the actions of his friends. They had never intended to hurt anyone. In fact, they justified the body snatching as necessary so that they might help people throughout their lives. The student also felt guilt as he plunged a hand in his pocket to touch the gold locket.

Satisfied that the body was not in the room, the searchers moved on. For only a moment the student breathed a sigh of relief. At least he personally could not be tied to the theft, but the searching team would soon reach the attic.

The sheriff finished searching the rooms and, with a good deal of encouragement from the grief-stricken father, asked if there were any other storage areas in the building. The campus staff replied that there was a storage area in the attic, but that it was not used because it was difficult to get to. One had to pull a set of stairs down out of the ceiling and climb the rickety steps. The girl's father would not overlook one possibility, so he insisted that the sheriff go into the attic.

The sheriff sent for a lantern to light his way on that dreary day, and then he helped to pull the creaky steps down so that he could mount them. He shifted his bulk through the narrow opening in the ceiling after he had set the lantern up on the floor of the attic. Holding the lantern high, he looked over the large empty space carefully. He then lowered himself and announced that there was nothing up there but dirt.

The searchers moved on but the dead girl's father was doomed to disappointment. His daughter's body was not to be recovered.

The young medical student who had the broken necklace thought about getting rid of it from time to time, but he never did. He could not bring himself to simply toss it away, and he did not relish returning to the attic and dropping it down after the body. So it simply moldered away among the doctor's personal possessions.

Years later, the doctor happened to learn that Chambers Hall, his old dormitory, was home to a strange story. Young men had been seeing a beautiful, dark-haired girl standing by a specific pillar at Chambers Hall for many years. Some of the young men had spoken to the girl while others were shocked to find that she disappeared as they approached. In fact, even faculty at the school had seen the ghostly girl. The students had named her Louise, and they always described her in the same terms. She was a lovely dark-haired girl, wearing outdated genteel clothing and a gold locket around her throat. She smiled softly and nodded to them before fading away. Mystery surrounded the girl, for no one knew who she was or why she seemed to hover near that one pillar in Chambers Hall.

When the doctor heard the story, he knew exactly who the girl was and why she haunted that area. He made inquiries and learned that the young man who now resided in his former dormitory room had several detailed experiences with Louise. The doctor managed a pretext for being introduced to the student and then asked him to dinner. As the medical student was ready to graduate within a few weeks, he accepted the dinner invitation happily. He was hoping that the old doctor would offer him a position in his practice. The doctor, though, had other reasons for the invitation. He skillfully maneuvered the conversation around to the mysterious ghostly girl of Chambers Hall. The medical student was not anxious to admit to seeing ghosts, but he gladly told stories of others who had seen the girl.

"And just how do they describe her?" queried the physician.

The medical student began to describe the girl and then said, "She has no jewelry evident except . . ."

Here the doctor interrupted. "Except a gold locket?"

The medical student paused in surprise. "Yes, except for a gold locket. How did you know?"

"Forgive me for answering your question with a question, but have you ever seen the girl?" The doctor pinned his gaze upon the young man.

The medical student hesitated and then sighed. "Indeed I have. I've spoken to her on several occasions. She never talked long, but she had a pleasant smile and I was shocked when I tried to linger with her and she simply faded away before my eyes."

The old doctor nodded and pulled something from his pocket. "The locket she wore, would you be able to recognize it if you saw it again?"

The medical student nodded. "Indeed, I could. It was quite an old-fashioned piece with gold filigree around it."

The doctor dangled the necklace he had withdrawn from his pocket. "Did it look like this?"

The medical student could not take his eyes off the locket. "Yes, it did. But how did you come by this? Did you know the girl?"

The doctor smiled ruefully. "Only in passing," he muttered. "But I do believe that I might be able to clear up a great deal of mystery for you, but only if you vow that you'll not reveal my identity. I am not worried for myself after all these years, but my crime was shared with others whom I would not like to cause problems."

The medical student gave his promise and the doctor began to tell his story. He spoke about the rash young men and about the pain of the bereaved father. He explained where the body had been secreted and that he had kept the locket for all those years.

"It was a foolish thing for us to have done, but we were drunk and young. We didn't think." The doctor concluded by placing the locket on the table. "It has been a secret for many years, but now the story should be told. You all call her Louise and I think it is time that everyone knows how her gentle spirit came to be there. You may tell the story but without any names."

The story was told and retold for many years. Louise was most active in the 1930s, when she appeared to countless students and faculty at Chambers Hall. She seems to have grown reticent over the years and is rarely seen near the pillar today. Her story, however, has become woven into the tapestry of the campus and she is remembered to every freshman class.

There is another version of the story that is lesser known, and in this version the corpse that was stolen was that of a beloved old black servant, whose body was secreted in the pillar for similar reasons. This version does not explain why Louise is seen, but it is possible that both stories bear a grain of truth since through the years many bodies were stolen for use at the college.

Santer Cats

The southern United States is honeycombed with strange tales of big cats. Some locals, especially in the eastern parts, call them Wampus Cats, but in North Carolina they were known as Santer Cats. Wampus Cats are commonly thought of as demons or monsters. Santers are simply mystery cats. Sightings of both Wampus and Santer cats seem to come in bunches, as if the creatures are traveling in and out of areas at certain times.

In the last half of the nineteenth century, a spate of Santer Cat stories circulated throughout the state. Researcher Angelo Capparello III discovered reports of them in old newspapers of the era.

Perhaps one of the best-documented series of sightings took place in Yadkin and Iredell counties in 1890. During that time the cats seemed to be quite active. In August of that year, people reported seeing a large feline with stripes from its nose to the tip of its tail. Other reports claimed that the cat was completely gray. The cat was seen predominately around Second Creek in Iredell County.

There are no known reports of Santer Cats in the area for nearly seven years after that time—nothing until March 1897, when another series of sightings began in Yadkin County, near the Roaring River area. For the next three years, the reports continued to come in sporadically. The Santer Cats wandered into the counties neighboring Yadkin and Iredell as well. People saw and heard them, but no one experienced any trouble with them.

What happened to the Santer Cats after that is a mystery. They did not reappear until May 1934, when reports came again from Iredell County. Once more, the cats minded their own business and no one reported any losses of livestock or pets due to the cats' presence.

Today, there are still big-cat sightings in the region, but the term Santer Cat is rarely used. Some folks believe the cats are migrating Florida panthers. Others feel it is a mysterious feline about which little is known.

The Angry Spirit of McIntosh Mine

Is it possible that a ghost has kept people away from a rich vein of gold for nearly two hundred years? Well, consider the following tale.

In the 1830s, the Charlotte region was gold mining country and sported several lucrative mines. One of those was the McIntosh Mine, located in southern Cabarrus County and known for the rich gold ore that it produced. It was also known as a dangerous mine because the owner, Skinflint McIntosh, was so cheap he cut corners when it came to shoring up the mine shafts.

When a vein of gold was found four hundred and fifty feet down a shaft one day, McIntosh was thrilled. He knew he would be one of the richest men in the area. But his workers were unwilling to risk their lives down a narrow, dangerous shaft.

McIntosh was livid that he had a fortune in the ground and no one to bring it up for him. There was a local miner named Joe McGee who was well known as one of the best in the business. Through the years, McIntosh had tried to hire Joe but he could never pay his price. Now McIntosh sent for Joe and said he wanted to hire him.

Joe considered the situation and sighed. "A man could get killed going down there," he said solemnly. "That wouldn't do my wife and kids any good."

"If you got killed down there, I'd give your wife a thousand dollars," McIntosh insisted. "You'd not have to worry about them."

Joe looked sharp. "Make it two thousand dollars and my price for digging and you've got a deal."

McIntosh was thrilled. "Two thousand dollars then if you get killed and the price of your hire as we have agreed," he affirmed.

With that Joe came to work for McIntosh. He worked night after night in the mine bringing up the gold. Soon, other men agreed to join Joe, for they trusted his judgment. Among those who joined him was an old friend named Shaun.

One night, Joe did fail to come home when his shift ended. His wife worried until late morning, when she made the trek to the mine. No one had seen Joe leave the mine shaft. To add to the worry, a series of small mine collapses occurred in an area that should have been vacant. For days the men hunted for Joe in the dark, twisty mine shafts, but they found nothing. At last Joe's wife approached McIntosh and told him that she needed the money promised on the paper Joe had signed. McIntosh scoffed. "I'll not be paying you because your man up and run off. There's not an ounce of proof he didn't come up from the shaft that night and just wander off himself. You'll get no money from me, woman!"

Weeks went by and the McGee family grew poorer and poorer. There was virtually nothing left and winter was already biting cold.

One night Joe's friend Shaun heard a pounding on his door and pulled it open. To his horror there stood the spirit of Joe McGee.

Joe looked tired and forlorn. "Have you found my body yet?" he asked faintly.

Shaun shook his head no.

"I'm buried under the green timbers that broke in the third side tunnel," Joe instructed. "Has McIntosh paid my family yet?"

Again Shaun shook his head. "No, Joe, he says he won't do it."

Suddenly Joe roared at Shaun. "You tell that Skinflint that I'll haunt his mine forever for cheating my family!" With that Joe faded away.

The next day Shaun passed the word about Joe's visitation and what he had said. The men dug at the spot that Joe indicated and they found the body. But even the body did not sway McIntosh to pay up.

After that, Joe kept his word. He appeared among the miners as they rode to work, and he walked among them all night. Before long, not a single man would work the mine anymore. No matter how much McIntosh offered to pay, he could not find anyone willing to brave Joe's wrath. Eventually he had to close the mine, leaving a vast fortune untapped. The mine was reopened briefly, but Joe put in a few appearances, and it was again quickly closed. Today, the gold is still down there somewhere, but only Joe McGee knows where to dig, and he doesn't want to see McIntosh's mine opened ever again.

Chaffin's Will

James L. Chaffin was a very fortunate man. He and his wife had raised four good sons—James P., Abner, Marshall, and John—who respected them and were hard-working men. Hard work was natural to them, because they had grown up helping their father farm the land.

Chaffin, however, seemed to favor one son above the others and that was his third son, Marshall. Chaffin favored Marshall so much that he made a will in 1905, leaving everything to him alone. He left not a penny nor an acre of ground to his other three sons. He did not even provide for his wife in the will.

The exact reasons why Chaffin made this extraordinary decision will never be known, but he would have cause to reconsider his decision. While reading his Bible, Chaffin came upon Genesis 27 and was moved by it. In that chapter, Jacob deceived his father Isaac into giving away his older brother Esau's birthright. The passages must have spoken to Chaffin, as his subsequent actions show.

In 1919, Chaffin had a second, more equitable will drawn up. This time his four sons shared all property equally and were charged with caring for their mother. Unaccountably, Chaffin did not have the will witnessed and never mentioned it to his family. Instead, he hid it in his father's old Bible at the point where Genesis 27 began. He then wrote a note telling the finder where to look for the document. This he sealed up in an inner pocket of his black overcoat, which he only wore for dress. He sewed the pocket shut and never told a soul about it.

Surely, Chaffin intended to complete the will and tell his family at some point, but on September 7, 1921, he died in an accidental fall. His family only knew of one will, and so they brought the document out and had it probated. That was the 1905 will, in which Marshall received everything. Though the rest of the family must have been hurt, they did not contest the will and Chaffin's apparent wishes were fulfilled.

James Chaffin did not rest comfortably, however, with the wrong will probated.

In 1925, James P. Chaffin, the son, began having strange dreams. In the dreams, his father appeared to him but was silent. James P. got the distinct impression that his elder was trying to communicate something to him. James then had a vision one night of his father standing at the foot of his bed. The old man wore his best overcoat. He pointed out the sewn-up pocket and said, "You will find my will in my overcoat pocket." He then vanished.

The next day, James P. asked his mother about the overcoat and found that she had given it to his brother John. On July 6, James visited John and asked if he might look at the overcoat. John fetched it for his brother and listened as James P. described his dreams and vision. The two brothers slit the threads to open the coat and found the note telling them where to find the second will. At this point, John and James P. realized how strange their tale

would be if they did find the will. They enlisted some neighbors as witnesses to the events. Then the boys went to their mother's home with the witnesses in tow.

Mrs. Chaffin retrieved her father-in-law's tattered Bible and handed it to her company. Inside they found that a special pocket had been made in Genesis Chapter 27 by folding the sheets of paper in a special manner. Inside that pocket was the will. According to North Carolina law, the will was valid and could be probated, because Chaffin made it obvious by virtue of the letter in the overcoat that he meant for this will to be recognized by the court.

The new will was filed, but things did not run smoothly at first. Marshall had died in the meantime, and his widow and son contested the new will. A trial was set to begin in December of that year. During the trial, the entire story of the ghostly visitations came out. The witnesses came forward to testify about going to the Chaffin homestead and watching as the sons found the second will. Other witnesses testified that the will was written in the elder Chaffin's own hand. In the end, Marshall's widow and son examined the will and dropped the case. They could see that it was old Chaffin's wish that the property be split equally.

James P. had no doubt about the outcome, though. About a week before the trial was to begin he had another dream in which his father came to him. The old man asked his son where the old will was and James P. took this to mean that the new will would be probated in the end.

Skeptics and critics have long scoffed at the notion that James P. had ghostly visitations from his father. They insist that he used an elaborate story to justify finding the new will. But others believe that old Chaffin did contact his son to make right a wrong he had committed long ago.

Dead or Alive?

There was once a mansion known locally in the Charlotte area as White Oaks. It was the home of a wealthy businessman named Jon Avery. Avery was a ladies' man and began an affair with a married woman of great prominence who lived nearby. Late at night, he would go for a walk in the gardens of the estate and secretly meet his married lover. The couple stole hours of pleasure in the wee hours of the night by the moonlight. During these trysts, his lover often sought reassurance that Avery truly loved her.

"Promise me," the woman cooed, "that you'll always meet me here like this."

Avery smiled and pulled his lover closer. "I promise that I will always meet you here my pet," he whispered back. "Dead or alive I will always come here for you."

It was a secret promise whispered in the dark, and no one would have known of it if not for subsequent events.

One day, Avery's mistress was attending a function. While socializing, she was asked if she had heard the news. Local gossip traveled rapidly and she leaned her head forward to catch this most recent bit.

"Haven't you heard," her informer inquired, "that Jon Avery of White Oaks passed away a week ago."

The mistress pulled away as if stung. "That's preposterous," she sputtered before realizing that she was making a bit of a scene. She could not go further and so excused herself.

The woman hurried home and sent a servant to inquire at White Oaks after Avery's health. When the servant returned with his report the woman literally fainted. It seemed that indeed the local gossip was correct and Avery had died more than a week earlier.

The mistress's collapse elicited the interest of her husband and friends. She confessed her affair and sobbed out a strange tale. It seemed that five days after Avery died, he kept an assignation with his mistress in the gardens. He had kept his word when he said that alive or dead he would meet her in the garden again.

The Ghosts of Gold Hill

After gold was first discovered in 1799, about twenty-five miles from Charlotte in Cabarrus County, many men decided to earn a living and perhaps make a fortune by mining for the precious metal.

One of those men was Aaron Klein, who took a job at the Randolph Mine on Gold Hill in the 1840s. He was a Jewish man whom many described as quiet and personable, but for others he was the butt of anti-Semitic jokes, which were slung at him daily. Aaron bent his back to his task and did not rise to the baiting. He had a plan for his life and he refused to be distracted by fools and bigots.

Aaron had a great affection for a young woman in town and she returned his love. He hoped to earn enough money to marry her and start a new life somewhere else. The work in the mine was a means to an end, and Aaron tried to remind himself of that when the taunts and pranks became especially bad.

There was one man who especially disliked Aaron. His name was Stan Cukla, and he also had feelings for Aaron's young woman. Stan seemed to think that if Aaron was out of the picture, the young woman would share those affections. So he drove Aaron mercilessly.

One day, Stan decided to set a trap for Aaron—a deadly trap. He told Aaron that the boss wanted to talk to him in the mine that night. When Aaron entered the 850-foot-deep mine, he saw Stan step out of the darkness. Suddenly, Stan pushed Aaron down the mine shaft. He left the mine, thinking his rival was gone and would soon be forgotten.

The next day, the mine boss was surprised when Aaron failed to show up for work, as he was a good and reliable worker. Three more days passed before the boss sent word around that he was looking for Aaron Klein. No one seemed to know what had become of the young man.

Only days after Aaron's disappearance, the men began talking about a strange golden light at the mouth of the mine shaft. It was a strange phenomenon, but the men continued working. But Stan began to worry about the light. It bothered him a lot. Was it Aaron's spirit coming back to tell of his misdeeds? He dreaded going to work and began talking to himself. He grumbled darkly about ghosts and spirits. Soon Stan was spending his breaks and free time digging around the bottom of the mine. He muttered and dug and seemed to get crazier with each passing day. No one bothered the strange fellow, for they knew he was sliding into madness.

One night, Stan again stayed after work to dig in the pit. Shortly after the other men left the mine and Stan was alone, there was a sudden rumble. A cloud of dust rose from the pit and the men froze. The mine had collapsed down at the base. When they finally dug down to Stan, he was dead and barely recognizable.

In the next few weeks, the men began to put the pieces together. Aaron Klein's angry spirit caused the collapse of the mine shaft to get revenge on the man who had killed him.

Gold Hill has at least one other ghost, or at least parts of the ghost. In January 1954, two miners claimed to have seen the disassembled body parts of a man floating near the old mine. The parts, including the head, were glowing softly in the darkness as the men watched them in horror. As the parts got closer, the men wanted to run, but then a terrific crack sounded and the mass disappeared.

Later, the men heard the story of Joe Newman, who had been the brother of the mine owner, Walter George Newman. Joe had been working in the mine several years earlier when there had been a terrible explosion, supposedly caused by gases seeping into it. At least that was the explanation Walter gave when folks mentioned the mine disaster that took his brother's life. Many people who knew the men thought that Walter killed Joe on purpose to gain full control of the mine. When Walter Newman died in 1918, people reported seeing him in and around the mine. It was believed the two brothers were still struggling for control of the mine.

Brothers House

When Andreas Kremser came to join the order of monks in Yadkin County, he was only sixteen years old. He was a German lad who enjoyed working with his hands, and through the years, he perfected his skills as a cobbler.

At middle age, Brother Andreas was a jovial soul who always wore a red jacket and smoked a pipe. He often whistled as he worked on his shoes. The monks were fond of him, as he was always ready to pitch in and help the community. Brother Andreas was called on to help dig out a wall for the basement of a new building. As he was laboring one day, the ground shifted and collapsed on him, burying him alive. The ground crushed his chest, and he died as soon as the painful pressure of the dirt was removed. All the brothers of the order mourned for their beloved friend.

Within days of Brother Andreas's death, a few of his brethren were walking along a hallway that led to the cobbler's shop. They heard footsteps overtake them, and then heard a whistle lilting along the way. The monks recognized the sound as it passed them. It was the exact tune that Brother Andreas used to whistle. But all doubt was left behind when they looked down the hall and saw a glimpse of his red jacket disappear around the corner.

For many years, people have reported hearing the sounds of a phantom working in the cobbler's shop. Others see a figure in a jaunty red jacket moving toward the shop. As in life, Brother Andreas is a good spirit, content to continue going about his work.

Old Salem Tavern

It was just after dark on a warm September night in 1831 when the stranger first entered the Salem Tavern. The man was badly injured and nearly unconscious, but instinct had driven him to the little town for help. The tavern keeper was shocked by the condition of the young man, and he immediately sent for the doctor. With the help of the servants, the tavern keeper got the stranger to bed. While the doctor took care of the man, the tavern keeper went through his clothes looking for any form of identification, but found nothing. By this time, the man had lapsed into a coma.

The doctor was not optimistic about the man's recovery and told the tavern keeper that nothing could be done for him, other than to make him comfortable. The tavern keeper and his employees nursed the fellow the best they could, but he soon died. On September 6, the stranger was laid to rest in a new cemetery, which is known today as Strangers Graveyard. No marker adorned his grave for there was nothing to put on one.

The tavern keeper gave little thought to the poor man afterward. He had fulfilled his Christian duty and saw that the man had a proper burial, but that was before his staff began to whisper that something had changed at the tavern.

Some of them hesitated about going to the basement, because they were hearing strange noises down there. The tavern keeper thought this was foolishness.

Then the staff began whispering about footsteps and shuffling sounds in the attic, where the tavern keeper had placed the stranger's possessions. Some said they began feeling cold breezes coming from the room where the stranger had died.

After a employee stormed from the attic one night, saying he confronted a ghost, the tavern keeper decided to put an end to the rumors by checking it out himself. He lit a lamp and went up the stairs. In the flickering light he could see the various bundles in storage. Looming old furniture created strange shadows, but there were no ghosts. Still, the space seemed frightening to him.

As the tavern keeper neared the doorway of the attic, a shadow separated from the wall and confronted him. In the flickering light he could see the face and shape of the stranger. The tavern keeper was frightened, but he had no recourse but to stand where he was or pass through the shade of the stranger.

The stranger began to speak and quickly thanked the tavern keeper for his kindness in his last days. He told him that his name was Samuel McClary and he was a businessman from South Carolina who had been on his way home when he had taken ill. He asked the tavern keeper to write to his fiancée and tell her where he was buried.

The tavern keeper promised, but once he got downstairs and calmed down he began to question himself. Had he actually talked to the ghost of the stranger or had the stress of the attic caused him to hallucinate?

For days, the tavern keeper did nothing. Then one night McClary appeared again, pleading with the tavern keeper to write to his fiancée and tell her where to find him. He gave him her address and then disappeared.

This time the tavern keeper wrote down the information. Foolish as it seemed, he decided to write to this mythical woman. He decided that only by doing so could he put his imagination to rest. Most probably the letter would be returned, but at least he could comfort himself by saying that he had tried.

Weeks passed after the letter was sent. As the tavern keeper was just putting the strange spirit out of his mind, a young woman arrived and asked for him. Clutched in her hand was the missive he had sent to her. She was the dead Samuel McClary's fiancée.

The tavern keeper told her about how McClary had arrived at his establishment and collapsed. He told her about caring for the fellow and about his burial. He even told her about the haunting, for she wondered how on earth he had found her. She thanked the tavern keeper for his many kindnesses

The young woman had her beloved exhumed and moved to another cemetery. The story of the stranger and the tavern keeper became public knowledge.

A similar story made the rounds in the late 1990s. In this version, the stranger was a Texan, and after he died his spirit sat on the roof of the tavern shouting out to the customers. The rowdy ghost kept up his shenanigans until the tavern keeper finally wrote to his brother to come and get his body.

Blue Ridge

THE NORTHERN PART OF THE BLUE RIDGE PROVINCE IS RICH IN HISTORY and ghostlore. The area is rough and mountainous and is often referred to as High Country or Land of the Sky. Many stories are set in the mountains that dominate the region, including romantic legends of Blowing Rock and the Devil's Stairs. But perhaps no other phenomenon is so uniquely part of the northern Blue Ridge as the ghostly chorus of Roan Mountain. From the southern Blue Ridge come tales that are older than the history of the first English settlers. Natives of the region have a vast lore stretching to the tragedy of the Trail of Tears. The story of one Cherokee man, Tsali, and the sacrifice he made is a sacred part of the region's history. The mountains are ever-present in the ghostly tales here as well, especially the romantic saga of the lovers of the Pisgah and the mysterious reports of monsters who lurk in the forests of this haunted land.

Yunwi Tsundi

The Cherokees' ties to western North Carolina run far back in time, long before European settlement. In their stories they tell of others who inhabited the lands who they called the Yunwi Tsundi, or the "Little People."

As the name denotes, the Yunwi Tsundi were very small. They only stood about two feet tall at the most. They wore their black hair long, letting it nearly touch the ground. With the exception of their height, they looked much like the Cherokee themselves. The Yunwi Tsundi were a gentle folk who loved to sing, dance, and play drums. It is said that the sound of their drumming can still be heard today on occasion if one listens carefully.

The Yunwi Tsundi were great neighbors to the Cherokee. Working only at night, they were known to gather corn or firewood for the winters. In times of distress, they offered their help and often left gifts of medicine when illness struck.

The Cherokee tried to stay on friendly terms with the Yunwi Tsundi, but on occasion someone would offend them. If they were insulted, they simply left and never returned. It was considered a terrible shame to lose such good neighbors.

When the first Europeans appeared in North Carolina, they did not believe in the Yunwi Tsundi, and they cared little about insulting them. They said the Yunwi Tsundi were myths, part of the Cherokee imagination. But the Cherokee could care less what others thought; the Yunwi Tsundi were old friends. Even today, some Cherokee assert that their little neighbors still exist, but they stay far away from society and civilization and take refuge in the wilderness retreats of long ago. On occasion, however, someone deep in the woods of western North Carolina claims to have seen the diminutive beings.

The Lovers Leap of Blowing Rock

Perhaps the most romantic spot in all of North Carolina is an area known as Blowing Rock, located where the Blue Ridge Mountains meet the Pisgah National Forest. It is said that Blowing Rock is the only place in this world where snow falls upside down. Clouds engulf Blowing Rock as it hangs thirty-five hundred feet above the Johns River Valley. Through the years, it has become a custom for people to drop lightweight items, such as handkerchiefs and hats, over the rim. Quite often, the wind rushing through the gorge offers enough of an updraft so that the dropped item will softly flutter upward back toward the one who discarded it.

Long ago, during the Great Removal, there lived a powerful Cherokee man named Osseo. When his beloved daughter, Wenonah, reached womanhood, he sent willow branches to all of the surrounding villages as a way of announcing that he would be receptive to marriage proposals. Wenonah's beauty and charm preceded her and several older men came to seek her hand. They spoke to her father of their brave deeds and how they would protect the young woman. They exhibited their wealth and made promises of how happy they would make Wenonah. Younger suitors played music or danced in brave pantomimes telling of old battles. Osseo found several of the men suitable and consulted Wenonah about her choice.

For Wenonah, there were two young men who caught her eye. Both were handsome and brave. This started a rivalry between the two men, and Osseo decided that there was only one way to sort out the dilemma. He set up a series of tests to see which of the men was stronger and more determined to have Wenonah's hand. The men were told to fight on the narrow cliff of Blowing Rock.

At the appointed time, the two men began their wrestling match on the narrow precipice. It was only at that moment that Wenonah realized that she did have feelings for one man over the other. She screamed out his name in an attempt to stop the foolhardy contest, but her screams distracted the men and the one she would have chosen stumbled and fell backward off of the cliff. The young man's screams tore at Wenonah's heart as she rushed forward to the very edge of the cliff. Osseo cried out the young woman's name at the last second and she stopped.

Wenonah dropped to her knees screaming out her pain as she tore her clothing and cried to the gods for help. In that one moment, her grief was so real and so raw that the gods heard her plea and lifted the young man back up through the air to the top of the cliff, where he fell safely to the ground at Wenonah's feet.

It is said that today when one throws an item over the cliff at Blowing Rock the wind picks up the item and carries it back upward in remembrance of Wenonah and her young love.

The Devil's Stairs

North Carolina has more than its share of ghostly spots, and one of the most haunted is the area known as the Devil's Stairs. Long before the first Europeans set foot in the area that is now part of Ashe County, the natives knew of the mysterious nature of the

Devil's Stairs. Their stories of the haunted mountain are lost to time, but a more modern tale lingers on.

In 1910, a miner working in the area was setting dynamite when a charge went off prematurely. The poor miner was blown up instantly. Shortly after his death, the other miners claimed to see him around the mineshaft walking up toward the Devil's Stairs. The spirit of the miner seemed oblivious to those watching him as he climbed the stairs and promptly disappeared.

But the miner was not the first ghost known to appear in the area. Shortly after the West Jefferson area was first settled, people talked about the Rider. Some folks passing by Devil's Stairs would say their horses reacted strangely in the area. A horse would suddenly stop, as if something had frightened it. As the traveler struggled to bring the horse under control, he felt someone slip up behind him on the horse's back. At that point, the horse went wild with fear. It was all that the hapless traveler could do to keep the horse from bolting and possibly killing them both. After they had passed by the Devil's Stairs, the traveler felt the invisible being slip off the horse and the beast calmed down. The identity of the mysterious Rider has been lost through time, but it was believed that someone haunted the area and was trying to find a way to leave it.

In time, the mine was abandoned and it became a spot where young people hung out to party or make out. But even they began to eschew the spot after a mentally ill girl took her newborn infant there and murdered it. Such a tragedy was bound to spawn ghostly tales, and it is said that on certain nights the thin cries of a newborn are heard.

The Ghostly Chorus of Roan Mountain

In Mitchell County sits Roan Mountain, a bald landform older than time. It sits at the northern edge of the Pisgah Forest and has been considered both a magical and sacred place. The Catawba Indians fought their battles there so that the gods would see their bravery. Through the years, there have been many stories about the windy mountain, but none is stranger than that of the Ghostly Chorus. The earliest documented encounter with the Ghostly Chorus was when John Strother, who was working on a survey team affixing the border between Tennessee and North Carolina, wrote about hearing the chorus in 1799. Strother described a odd phenomenon in his journals that began with a devilish wind that battered the mountainside. The wind became so strong that it blew the clouds round and round. Finally, he heard what sounded like a chorus singing a horrible dirge. He could not make out the words, but the sound of voices seemed unmistakable to him.

Through the years people settled on Roan Mountain. Among them was General John T. Wilder, who built a lodge on the mountain in 1877, and then the much larger Cloudland Hotel in 1885. Wilder, his staff, and his guests witnessed the devilish wind and the mournful song of the Ghostly Chorus. Though the view from Roan Mountain was awe-inspiring, the hotel failed because the cost to keep such a remote spot in business became too high. Some say, however, it was also because of the terrible wailing heard on the mountain.

One of Wilder's guests, a man named Henry Colton, decided to locate the source of the music. He enlisted the aid of two other guests and Wilder himself. One night the wind blew up in its strange circular fashion and became especially difficult to withstand. The men hurried outside and waited for the sound of the phantom chorus to begin. Shortly thereafter, they heard the wailing song rising up all around them. Colton attempted to locate the direction of the song but was unable to do so. Through the years Colton considered many theories, but none seemed right. Though the wind often accompanied it, the chorus could be heard even after the wind died down. All that he could ascertain is that whatever the source, the music did have a lyrical tone that seemed beyond random chance.

Another guest of Wilder's named Pere Libourel also set out to discover the source for the ghostly sound. Libourel was a young man of science who was confident that he knew exactly what was going on. He believed that the strange circular wind was the source of the sound. He explained that it must be the wind blowing through the treetops. He set out to prove his theory, despite the warnings from Wilder to be careful not to get lost in the massive forest. He trotted off dressed for his hike and carrying a long stick he had picked up the day before and followed the wind around to the source.

When Libourel was found the next day, he was wandering along and babbling rather incoherently. His clothing was badly torn, but he was still clutching his precious walking stick. As he recovered, he made a fantastic claim. He insisted that the circular wind had driven him into the side of a cliff, where a cave had suddenly opened up behind him. The wind tore at his clothing and battered him with tree branches, until he was obliged to seek shelter within the strange little cave. But he found the cave to be a terrible, fearsome place filled with the wailing of the spirits within. The sound wrapped around him and he shuddered as he saw the spectral chorus for a few seconds before he blacked out.

Libourel described what he saw and shuddered with horror. Human figures badly malformed or torn apart appeared before him. He could see broken bones, missing limbs, and seeping wounds. The figures were garbed in tattered clothing. They clambered and wailed. He was sure that these were the lost souls of hell wailing in the mountain for eternity.

Libourel was forced to pause there until the wind died down and he could stumble from the cave. When he felt the freshness of the air again, it was damp from rain. A rainbow of amazing color was spread over the mountain.

Later Libourel tried to lead others to the cave, but where he had seen it there was only a solid rock face. He would have thought he was in the wrong place, except there was a bit of cloth from his shirt firmly stuck in a sharp rock. His fellow guests shook their heads and said Libourel's encounter was the result of his having struck his head. It was all a dream, they laughed.

Locals have long told another less ghastly tale. They claim that angels are the source of the Ghostly Chorus and that the rainbows they occasionally glimpse are God's halo shining on his servants. But others who have heard the sound of the Ghostly Chorus dispute that angels could ever make such a lonesome sound.

Tsali's Sacrifice

Tsali never thought he would become a hero. He and his people had lived on the Nantahala River, not far from what is today called Bryson City, for many years. Tsali was a traditionalist, because he kept to the old ways. He farmed and hunted to support his family.

All he wanted was to live with his wife and three sons in the mountains and be left alone.

For years, the government had been trying to remove the Cherokee from North Carolina, Alabama, Georgia, and Tennessee. Tsali and more than a thousand others in his tribe were first sent outside the boundaries of the Cherokee Nation in an area called Quallatown. Then, in May 1838, Tsali's brother-in-law brought word that General Winfield Scott was bringing seven thousand soldiers to force the Cherokee to the western lands. He told Tsali that by the next new moon, all Cherokee would begin the long march. Twenty-five stockades had been built to pen the Cherokee people until the time when the great march began. It was not long before the soldiers came for Tsali and his family.

On that morning, Tsali was in the fields when soldiers led by Lieutenant A. J. Smith rounded up his wife and sons and also his brother-in-law, sister, and their family. They were told they were being taken to Fort Bushnell to await the journey westward. There were four armed soldiers and at least one of them was on horseback. Tsali and his family offered no resistance. The families hastily gathered up supplies, but it was a meager amount for a family to live on.

After their time at Fort Bushnell, Tsali's family began the long walk in June 1838. Tsali was angered time and again by the insolence of the soldiers and the quick pace they were forced to take, which did not account for the children, the elderly, and the ill. People collapsed and many were dying, but the soldiers showed no mercy. The federal government under President Andrew Jackson determined that the Cherokee should be moved to a territory that is today Oklahoma.

According to the Cherokee version of the story, the soldiers were not polite and kept prodding the families to hurry. One of the soldiers jabbed Tsali's wife between the shoulders with a bayonet to prod her onward. At this point, Tsali had enough. He spoke to his brother-in-law and other men that night and decided that on the next day they would make a suicide run against the soldiers and flee into the hills with their families. It would be better to die trying to protect themselves than being led like sheep to their deaths. Tsali's words moved the men. The soldiers knew that the Indians were talking, but none of them understood Cherokee, so they were unaware what was afoot. Word spread quickly among the people

about what would happen on the morrow.

The next day, Tsali waited for the right time. His group was traveling in a little band with only four soldiers directly responsible for them. At the appointed moment, the men sprang forward and grabbed at the guns. One of the soldiers engaged them in a tussle and his gun fired, shooting the soldier in the head. At that point the other soldiers fled.

In Lieutenant Smith's version of the story, one of the Cherokee men drew a small ax and threw it at one of the soldiers, burying it in his skull. Smith admitted that the soldier had prodded an old woman, but that it was not provocation for the attack. Subsequently, General Scott dispatched Colonel William Foster to hunt down the murderers with the order to execute all those involved.

Some of the terrified people, led by Tsali, escaped into the foothills. Tsali and his band lived at Clingman's Cave on Deep Creek for some time. Some of the runaway Cherokee were captured and three of them were shot. Tsali, however, lingered in the mountains. The soldiers knew of their whereabouts and used a lawyer and trader named Will Thomas, who had lived among the Indians, to speak to them. General Scott promised that if the Tsali band turned itself in, the Cherokee could return to Quallatown.

Thomas sent word to the band, and when Tsali heard the words of Scott, he sent word that he and his family would surrender. The others in his band could make their own decision.

Tsali turned himself in, along with his family and his brother-in-law's family. A female missionary at the post realized what was about to happen. She hurried to the commander and shamed him by pointing out that one of Tsali's sons was just a boy. She begged him for the boy's life in the name of God, saying they could not execute a child, The woman managed to have Tsali's youngest son spared, along with his wife. The rest were tied up and executed.

On November 24, 1838, Colonel Foster reported that the principles directly responsible for the murder were dead. He further indicated that he did not believe Tsali to be responsible for the death. Instead he said that Tsali's brother-in-law, Nantayalee George, and Tsali's son, Nantayalee Jake, were the guilty ones. He based his assertions upon the testimony of Will Thomas, who had spoken to those involved. Despite Foster's report, Tsali was executed.

It is said that up on the mountain where he once lived, Tsali is still seen roaming free. He has cheated the whites who tried to drive him out, for now he wanders where his spirit desires and there is nothing that can be done about it.

The Lantern Bearer

For Ella and Lois, late nights in fall were long and harrowing. The two young women had become friends after marrying two brothers. Neither woman liked to spend time alone, but when hunting season came they were forced to do just that. Their husbands had to go hunt deer to help their families survive the coming winter, but that did not make the closing of darkness around their Murphy-area homes any easier for them.

During this particular hunting trip in the mid-twentieth century, the women agreed to stay together. That way neither one had to deal with the loneliness that the darkness brought. They looked upon it as an adventure or a slumber party, and they stayed up late talking and laughing.

When Ella and Lois finally fell asleep, they were startled awake by the alarm clock going off. Lois jumped up, realizing that she was late for her journey home. By 5:00 A.M. each morning, she had to be out in the barnyard tending the livestock. The journey back home would be long and difficult, for it was a cold winter's morning and she shuddered as she stepped outside and felt the embrace of the bitter air. She ran to her car and started it up hoping that the heater would kick in soon.

Lois pulled on the button for the headlights, which flared up and cast an eerie glow into the darkness. She put her foot on the gas pedal and the car rolled forward on to the old gravel road. Slowly and carefully, she drove along the road as she tried to avoid the many ruts and potholes that pockmarked it. She was only about three miles from Ella's home when she first saw a man walking along.

At first, Lois only glimpsed the man moving in the distance. Then she could see that he had a golden glow about him. She could not help but think that the man appeared to be carrying a lantern of all things, and that made little sense to her. The man seemed to give no sign that he realized that Lois was behind him, and she had to put on the brakes.

Lois bit her lip as she waited for the man to move out of the middle of the road, but he still ignored her. At last she brought the heel of her hand down hard on the horn and jumped herself at the loudness of the sound. To her shock, the man did not turn to look at her or move in any way. It was as though he were oblivious of her.

A sudden fear gripped Lois's heart and she began to ease her foot down on the gas slowly and gently move along. It was as though she were afraid to stop the car completely. She could not tell why she was afraid, but she knew that stopping the car was dangerous.

Lois inched along behind the man, who still seemed unaware of her presence, and she fought against the fear that seemed to squeeze down on her. In the steady glow from her headlights, she made out that the man was old. Something about the man's movements seemed chilling to the young woman, and she would have sped past him if he had not blocked the road.

Lois began to think of turning back or finding a wide spot in the road so that she could suddenly rush past the old man. She could not have told anyone why she felt such great fear from a simple old man walking along, but she did.

Suddenly, the man disappeared. Lois blinked and rubbed her eyes. He had simply faded into the darkness. Lois flipped her headlights on high beam, but the man was nowhere to be found in the gloom of the early morning. She jammed her foot on the gas and sped ahead, unconscious of anything that was around her.

It was daylight by the time Lois completed her journey to her house, but she still shuddered as she sat in her warm car and remembered the slow shambling figure of the old man. Who was he? She wondered. Where did he come from? What was he doing on the road at 5:00 A.M. just walking down the middle of the road carrying a lantern?

In the days to come, Lois thought often of her strange encounter on the road, but it was some time before she came across a probable answer to her questions. Only years later would she learn that in the early 1900s, an old man's body had been found on the road near her encounter with the lantern bearer. It was said that the body had been found on a cold, late fall morning during hunting season and that the man had been shot twice and left for dead. Near the body of the poor murdered man, the police found a broken lantern, which he probably brought with him to light his path into the woods that morning as he went out to hunt. Strangely, no one ever identified the old man and no weapon was found near the body. Although Lois was the only one to see the old man, she was convinced that she had seen the spectral form of a man who had died almost fifty years earlier.

The Ghostly Lovers of the Pisgah

Jim Stratton was seventeen years old the first time he ever really looked at Mary Robinson. She had just turned fifteen. They were at a revival meeting up in the Pisgah Mountain territory. Jim had seen Mary before, but she never caught his eye until that night. She had dark hair and eyes that flashed like lightning at Jim. Her pale complexion made her look like a fine porcelain doll, and Jim was enthralled. For her part, Mary knew well who Jim Stratton was. All the mountain girls had an eye for the tall, broad-shouldered youth. He had dark hair that fell boyishly over his forehead and black eyes that danced when he laughed. He was strong and handsome, and he could work a full day as good as any man.

Jim began to manufacture reasons why he needed to go to the Robinson place. He was there on business, his mother wanted to borrow corn meal, and so on. Jim also used the still he ran as a reason why he needed to visit the Robinsons. Both Mary's father and Jim, like many men on the mountain, ran stills. It was a crime, but for mountain people in the early 1900s it was simple economics. They fought the hard-scrabble ground for enough corn to sell, but dried corn did not bring much money. Corn liquor, on the other hand, increased their profits many times over. For a man barely surviving, it was simply an economic decision to risk jail and sell corn liquor so that his family could survive.

Jim and Mary often found an opportunity to speak. He came to realize that Mary was not only one of the prettiest girls on the mountain, she was also smart. She had a native kind of wisdom that was born of living a hard life. She was also a good girl who in all things had always honored her mother and father.

By the time old man Robinson saw the way of things, Mary and Jim were deeply in love. Mary's father had dreams of something better for his girl, and so he was determined to break up the budding romance. He took the boy aside and told him point blank that he would forbid any relationship between the two.

Mary tried to talk sense to Jim, but he ignored it. Despite Mary's sensible words, she always hurried to meet Jim when she found him around the farm. They agreed to meet at a secret spot when he let out a certain bird call. Jim came as often as possible, calling for Mary with his bird sounds. Mary made excuses to hurry into the woods and made her way to Jim. Months went by and cold weather came. Jim and Mary still met in secret, but Mary tried to persuade Jim to slow down the romance. One cold winter's night in December when Jim met Mary, she found him very upset. Word had reached him that the next day revenue agents were going to raid his still. Hatred marred Jim's face that night. Mary's father was rumored to have been the person who turned him in. Old man Robinson would pay for his interference and his treachery, Jim vowed to his shaken Mary. Mary was torn between those she loved, and she counseled Jim to just go away for a while. She promised she would wait for him, but Jim shook his head grimly. He wanted to see this through.

The next day, Jim hid up the valley from his still and waited. In his hands was an ancient shotgun. Not knowing what he was going to do, he watched the government men smash his still and all of his stock. Then a terribly desperate anger welled up in him. To them it was just law, but for Jim it was his livelihood. Finally, the men picked up the twisted copper piece called the worm and they started down the mountain. Jim thought of how difficult it had been to save the money to buy that worm. He felt his hands grip the gun and raise it up. He then leveled it and pulled the trigger. The man carrying the copper tubing sagged to the ground. Jim was now a killer.

Terror filled Jim's heart and he ran from the scene. He ran until he made it to the cabin of Peggy Higgins, which was near his home. She and Jim had been friends for a long time. Jim had often helped the old widow with chores after she was unable to manage on her own. Now he told her his story.

Widow Higgins shuddered in fear for her friend. He needed to get away from the mountain fast, and she told him so, but Jim had other plans. He wanted to take his revenge on Mary's father and to steal her away. He begged Widow Higgins to help him. Against her better judgment, the old woman agreed. Jim told Widow Higgins to run and get Reverend Ball from down the mountain. He told her that he had something he needed to do and that he would be back at her cabin in two hours with Mary in tow.

Widow Higgins started off as fast as she could go. She worried and fretted, but there was little else that she could do. The wind and snow buffeted the old woman, yet she felt she could not turn back and let down her friend.

Jim headed for the Robinson place. He was dressed poorly for a long sojourn in the cold, but he refused to let his numb fingers and frozen feet keep him. He tried to decide what he would do once he reached the cabin. He imagined he would stand before the Robinson cabin and call out Mary's father. He wondered if he should give the old man a fair chance or just shoot him outright. Jim also imagined how Mary would react. Perhaps he should call out Mary and send her on her way before shooting her father.

At the cabin, he gave the bird cry and Mary came bursting out. She was in tears and warned him away. The revenue men had already checked the cabin and they were out for blood. Mary's father had gone with them to hunt Jim. In fact, he was going to try to round up a posse to help in the hunt. They were going to try and take Jim in dead or alive. Mary begged Jim to run.

Jim grabbed Mary's hands and stilled her. "Come away with me. I sent old Widow Higgins to fetch the preacher, and we can get married at her cabin. Then she'll help us escape. She's been a good friend for a long time and she'll help us."

The pleading in his voice and the love in his eyes undid Mary and she faltered. She so wanted to be Jim's wife. Was it possible that even now they could salvage a life from this horrible experience? Mary ran back into the house, grabbed a few things, and flung them into a shawl. She then bundled up in a heavy wrap. No pleading from her mother and siblings could stop her, and her mother understood that this might be the last time she saw her daughter.

Jim waited out in the bitter cold. In his heart he was relieved that Mary's father had already gone. If he had seen the man he would have killed him and how would Mary have felt about him after that? He just hoped to never lay eyes on the old man again or he would take his revenge despite Mary.

The cold and the fear prohibited the young lovers from talking, but the two stumbled through the snow and made it back to Widow Higgins's cabin. Jim crept up and checked it out before he called to Mary to enter. The cabin was still warm from the fire in the grate and Jim stirred it up. Widow Higgins was not back yet.

The young couple sat in the dwindling light waiting and starting at every noise. They talked about their coming life. Mary wondered if Reverend Ball was not been home, or if he had refused to venture out in the cold. Jim assured her that they could leave the mountain and find another preacher.

Widow Higgins eventually came stumbling in. She was sprinkled with snow and behind her came Reverend Ball. He knew the entire story and was wise enough to know that he would be unable to change the situation. He needed to hurry so that the young couple could flee.

The widow dug in a chest and brought out a yellowed wedding gown. She pressed it into Mary's hands. "Slip it on, child," she instructed. "A gal should have something special on her wedding day. I was married in this and now it's yours." Mary had no time to admire the ancient lace and the delicate fabric. She hurried to change and when she stepped back into the main room she would have been a vision except for the fear that marred her eyes.

"Do you have a ring?" the preacher asked. Jim shook his head.

"I don't, preacher," he confessed.

Widow Higgins fingered her own wedding band and looked down. She pulled it off and smiled softly. "Yes you do, Jim. Mary's being married in my gown and veil and I'd be honored if you'd use my ring. It stood my husband and I in good stead for many a year." She pressed the ring into Jim's hand. The look of gratitude in Jim's eyes was payment enough for this sacrifice, the old woman thought.

Within seconds, the ceremony began. Haste was needed and all of those assembled in the crude cabin felt it keenly. The preacher hurried but he was not quick enough. Dogs began barking far off, so the preacher finished quickly

Mary dashed to gather her things and Jim checked out the situation. The revenue men and the posse were coming up the trail to the widow's house. Jim and Mary's only chance was to slip out the back.

The young couple did not linger to thank the old woman, but she sent her blessings with them. The pounding on her door sounded only moments after the couple left, and the widow called out to them to wait while she lit a lamp. Darkness had fallen and with it came a heavy blanket of snow. She was surprised to see that the snow was now over knee-deep and was still falling menacingly.

Widow Higgins and the preacher stalled the men for a long time. She told them that Jim often came to her cabin and that was why the dogs had led them there. Darkness and hunger made the men less willing to push on. The old woman made a pot of soup and several of the men decided to spend the night before her hearth. Two men went with Mr. Robinson back to his cabin and two others followed the preacher just in case the young couple might try to contact him later.

It was a long and terrible night for Widow Higgins. She had slept very little. In her old bed she had prayed silently long into the night that Jim and Mary were safely away. She thanked the Lord for the heavy blanket of snow that now covered their tracks and made the dogs' job almost impossible. By the time the men stirred at first light, the snow was nearly waist-high. No one would be doing much traveling that day.

The men left the cabin for a while, but when they returned they told the old woman that tracking was almost impossible. They thought they had found a faint trail, but it led up into Pisgah Mountain and it was untraceable without shovels. No one could have survived to make it up there without tools in that snow. Their words froze Widow Higgins's heart.

Late that day, the town constable came and took the widow aside. He told her that the preacher had confessed what had happened. The constable said that he would not make a fuss about their parts in the affair, but that he feared Jim and Mary were dead. No one could have survived that storm and made it off the mountain. He was calling off the search until spring thaw.

When spring thaw did arrive, men combed the mountain for weeks, but no one found a thing. For Peggy Higgins's part, she was left to wonder what had happened to the young folks she had helped.

Mr. Robinson was a broken man. He no longer made moonshine. He barely worked, and the family became impoverished. What little money he had he spent on notices placed in newspapers asking for information on the whereabouts of his Mary. He never recovered from the shock of his loss.

The winter after Jim and Mary disappeared, people came down off Pisgah Mountain excited and upset. They claimed that as they walked they saw in the distance a young woman in a wedding dress and veil and a poorly attired young man. The young couple struggled against the snows as they held hands and hurried on. No matter how hard people tried to catch up to them, however, they were unable to do so.

Some people claimed to see the young bride in her wedding dress sitting wearily in the snow while her young groom hunkers down holding her hand, as if letting her rest before they had to go. The story of Mary and Jim never faded away and the young lovers have become part of the mountain where they had loved so long ago.

The Boojum of Haywood County

New Jersey has the Jersey Devil and West Virginia has the Mothman, but few know that a strange and fearful creature lives on Eagle Mountain in the Plott Balsams of Haywood County. The creature is called the Boojum, and its origins have been traced back to the very first written accounts from the area. The beast is described as a cross between a human and a bear. It is massive, has brown fur, and it issues a strange moaning sound. This beast, however, is fond of shiny objects and spends its time collecting rare mountain gems such as amethysts, rubies, emeralds, and beryl.

Stories of the Boojum go far back in time, but it was not until the Eagle's Nest Hotel was built on the mountain in the late 1800s that the story became part of the fabric of North Carolina. Stories of guests seeing the beast spread until it became popular to set up hunts for the creature. Although there is no record of any such creatures killed, many guests came away with stories of seeing the beast moving through the brush.

Locals know a good bit more about the Boojum. They know, for instance, that the beast is curious about humans, especially women. Through the years, young females who have gone bathing in the cool mountain streams often reported seeing the beast standing along the edge of the water staring at them. The beast often sighed or made grunting and moaning noises, and it was only when it made a sound that it was discovered. The beast would quickly hurry off when it realized that it had been seen. Others told of young women picking berries or taking strolls on the mountain who were approached by the beast in a tentative manner.

In the early 1900s, a young mountain girl named Annie encountered the Boojum, but she did not find the homely creature loathsome. When it approached her, she did not scream. She found something compelling in the gentle dark eyes and held out her hand to it. Thus began a friendship that blossomed into love. The mountain girl took the beast to heart and they were married in some fashion. Though the girl had a small cabin, where she would occasionally linger, she spent most of her time in the shelters that the Boojum chose. The Boojum, though, could not help its fascination with sparkling things and often wandered off for days at a time looking for gems. Annie went after the beast calling to him until he responded in his guttural way and she found him once more.

No one knows what became of Annie and the Boojum. Did they have children? Where and when did they die? It is believed that the couple must have had offspring, for Boojum are still reported in the area every now and then. It is said by some that late in her life Annie brought a bundle of Boojum's gems back to her family to help them out. Others say that the gems were buried shortly before Annie's death and that now she watches over them as a spirit in the woods.

The Spirit Rider

Near the old Calvary Episcopal Church in Fletcher, which is on U.S. Highway 176, a ghostly woman riding her palomino horse first appeared during the Civil War. It is said that at least one Union general believed that this ghost was responsible for no less than the deaths of twenty-three of his men.

It was early in 1865 when General George Stoneman and his troops were patrolling the area of Fletcher. Stoneman had sent out a scouting party one evening. Later on, a few men from the group came straggling back to the camp. Some were wounded and some were in shock. The survivors told Stoneman that they had been riding along when they saw a young woman on a palomino horse. The woman refused to stop when they called for her to halt. Instead, she turned the horse and took off at a gallop. The men pursued her, thinking that she must have been doing something illegal. They followed her down the road near the old church and beyond it a little way. The girl on the horse drew up suddenly and faded before the eyes of the startled men. Before they had time to react, the patrol was set upon by Confederates who opened fire on them. The girl had led the men right into an ambush.

General Stoneman was furious when he heard the story. The business about the girl disappearing was simply a trick by the rebels, he asserted. He garnered a good description of the girl and the horse from the survivors and ordered his men to search for her. He wanted the girl punished for the deaths of twenty-three of his men.

The Union soldiers began to search the surrounding area. People were questioned and a search was made for the palomino horse. On several occasions, Union soldiers came across the girl riding her horse along the same area where the ambush had occurred. They gave chase both times, but were cautious lest they end up like their brethren. Both times the girl managed to elude them. On at least three occasions, the Union soldiers shot at the girl as she fled from them. The soldiers were close enough each time to hit her, but the bullets did not faze the girl. They seemed to whiz through her as she faded into the night.

Eventually Stoneman questioned several local people who recognized the description of the girl and the horse. They each told the general that he had to be mistaken, for the horse and rider he claimed to have seen were dead. They told the general that a local woman had died of grief only a couple of years earlier. She had taken ill after learning that her husband had been killed by Union forces. The woman never recovered from the shock and in weeks she died.

Whether Stoneman believed the ghost story or not is unknown, but he did call off the hunt for the woman soon after learning the story. It is believed that the young woman's spirit deliberately led those Union soldiers into an ambush in retribution for what had happened to her husband. The rage apparently has not eased according to some people, for there are still reports of her riding her horse along the road near the church late at night.

Bibliography

Books and Articles

Austin, Sherry. *Mariah of the Spirits and Other Southern Ghost Stories*. Johnson City, TN: Overmountain Press, 2002.

Barefoot, Daniel W. *Seaside Spectres*. North Carolina's Haunted Hundred, vol. 1. Winston-Salem, NC: John F. Blair, 2002.

———. *Piedmont Phantoms*. North Carolina's Haunted Hundred, vol. 2. Winston-Salem, NC: John F. Blair, 2002.

———. *Haints of the Hills*. North Carolina's Haunted Hundred, vol. 3. Winston-Salem, NC: John F. Blair, 2002.

———. *Haunted Halls of Ivy: Ghosts of Southern Colleges and Universities*. Winston-Salem, NC: John F. Blair, 2004.

Berlitz, Charles. *Charles Berlitz's World of the Incredible but True*. New York: Fawcett Crest, 1991.

Burchill, James V., Linda J. Crider, Peggy Kendrick, and Marcia Wright Bonner. *Ghosts and Haunts from the Appalachian Foothills: Stories and Legends*. Nashville: Rutledge Hill Press, 1993.

Capparella, Angelo, III. "The Santer: North Carolina's Own Mystery Cat?" *North American BioFortean Review* II, no. 2 (2000).

Garrison, Webb. *A Treasury of Carolina Tales*. Nashville: Rutledge Hill Press, 1988.

Godfrey, Linda S. *Hunting the American Werewolf*. Madison, WI: Trail Books, 2006.

Guiley, Rosemary Ellen. *The Encyclopedia of Ghosts and Spirits*. 3rd ed. New York: Facts on File, 2007.

Harden, John. *The Devil's Tramping Ground and Other North Carolina Mystery Stories*. Chapel Hill: University of North Carolina Press, 1953.

———. *Tar Heel Ghosts*. Chapel Hill: University of North Carolina Press, 1980.

Hauck, Dennis William. *Haunted Places: The National Directory*. 2nd ed. New York: Penguin Books, 2002.

Holzer, Hans. *Real Hauntings: True American Ghost Stories*. New York: Barnes and Noble, 2002.

Jarvis, Sharon, ed. *The Uninvited*. True Tales of the Unknown, vol. 2. New York: Bantam Books, 1989.

Lacey, T. Jensen. *Amazing North Carolina*. Chattanooga, TN: Jefferson Press, 2008.

Kermeen, Frances. *Ghostly Encounters: True Stories of America's Haunted Inns and Hotels*. New York: Warner Books, 2002.

Mead, Robin. *Haunted Hotels: A Guide to American and Canadian Inns and Their Ghosts* Bolton, ON: Fenn and Company, 1995.

Morgan Fred T. *Ghost Tales of the Uwharries*. Winston-Salem, NC: John F. Blair, 2007.

Norman, Michael, and Beth Scott. *Haunted America*. New York: Tor Books, 2007.

———. *Historic Haunted America*. New York: Tor Books, 2007.

Preik, Brooks Newton. *Haunted Wilmington and the Cape Fear Coast*. Wilmington, NC: Stuart House.

Reevy, Tony. *Ghost Train!: American Railroad Ghost Legends*. Lynchburg, VA: TLC Publishing, 2001.

Roberts, Nancy. *America's Most Haunted Places*. Orangeburg, SC: Sandlapper Publishing, 1987.

———. *North Carolina Ghosts and Legends*. Columbia, SC: University of South Carolina Press, 1991.

———. *Civil War Ghost Stories and Legends*. Columbia, SC: University of South Carolina Press, 1992.

———. *Haunted Houses: Chilling Tales from 24 American Homes*. 3rd ed. Guilford, CT: Globe Pequot, 1998.

Russell, Randy, and Janet Barnett. *Mountain Ghost Stories and Curious Tales of Western North Carolina*. Winston-Salem, NC: John F. Blair, 1988.

Steiger, Brad. *Real Ghosts, Restless Spirits, and Haunted Places*. Canton, MI: Visible Ink Press, 2003.

Taylor, Troy. *Spirits of the Civil War: A Guide to the Ghosts and Hauntings of America's Bloodiest Conflict*. Alton, IL: Whitechapel Productions Press, 1999.

Toone, Emily, and Joseph Toone. *Cape Fear's Haunting Women*. Self-published, 2003.

Warren, Joshua P. *Haunted Asheville*. Asheville, NC: Shadowbox Publications, 1996.

Whedbee, Charles Harry. *Pirates, Ghosts, and Coastal Lore: The Best of Judge Whedbee*. Winston-Salem, NC: John F. Blair, 2004.

Zepke, Terrance. *Ghosts of the Carolina Coasts: Haunted Lighthouses, Plantations, and Other Historic Sites*. Sarasota, FL: Pineapple Press, 1999.

———. *Best Ghost Tales of North Carolina*. 2nd ed. Sarasota, FL: Pineapple Press, 2006.

Bibliography

Online Sources

Barnes, Roy. "Searching for the Lake Norman Monster Called 'Normie' in North Carolina." *Associated Content*. May 13, 2008. www.associatedcontent.com/article/760363/searching_for.

Book Rags. www.BookRags.com.

Brown Mountain Lights. www.brownmountainlights.com.

"The Cherokee in Graham County." *Graham County North Carolina Chamber of Information*. www.grahamchamber.com/cherokee.html.

Coleman, Loren. "Mitchell River Monster?" *Cryptomundo*. Posted May 2, 2006. www.cryptomundo.com/cryptozoo-news/mitchellrm.

Daily Advance. www.dailyadvance.com.

Devilstrampingground.com. www.devilstrampingground.com.

"Did You Say (gulp!) G-g-ghosts?" *Insiders' Guide*. www.insiders.com/wilmington/sb-kidstuff.htm.

Fort Fisher. www.ah.dcr.state.nc.us/sections/hs/fisher/fisher.htm.

Ghost Stories of North Carolina. www.ibiblio.org/ghosts.

"Haunted Houses and Haunted Places in North Carolina." *Real Haunts*. www.realhaunts.com/haunted-houses/united-states/north-carolina.

"Haunted Sites of North Carolina." *WelcomeToNC.com*. www.welcometonc.com/category/Hauntings.

"A History of the King's American Regiment." *The On-Line Institute for Advanced Loyalist Studies*. www.royalprovincial.com/military/rhist/kar/kar1hist.htm.

"Index to King's American Regiment History." *The On-Line Institute for Advanced Loyalist Studies*. www.royalprovincial.com/military/rhist/kar/karlist.htm.

Inman, Randy. "North Carolina Ghost Stories Just in Time for Halloween." *Associated Content*. October 19, 2006. www.associatedcontent.com/article/72989/north_carolina_ghost_stories_just_in.html

"Is Bentonville Haunted?—Plus Paranormal Activity at the Harper House." *Ghost Hunting Secrets*. http://ghosthuntingsecrets.com/blog/wp-trackback.php?p = 24.

"Kings Mountain." *National Park Service*. www.nps.gov/kimo.

Kirk, Lowell. "The Cherokee Legend of 'Tsali.'" *Angelfire*. www.angelfire.com/wv/cherokeeindian/page2.html.

Lake Norman Monster. www.lakenormanmonster.com/home.shtml

"North Carolina Ghost Stories and Folk Tales." *American Folklore*. www.americanfolklore.net/folktales/nc1.html.

"North Carolina Ghosts." *Haunted Travels: A Guide to Haunted Places*. www.hauntedtravels.com/north_carolina_ghosts.htm.

"North Carolina Legends and Ghost Stories." *North Carolina Department of the Secretary of State*. www.secstate.state.nc.us/kidspg/legends.htm

North Carolina Paranormal Research and Investigations. www.hauntednc.com.

"Overmountain Victory National Historic Trail: Patriot Troops at King Mountain." *National Park Service*. www.nps.gov/ovvi/troops.htm.

Tales from the Coast. www.coastalguide.com/tales.

Taylor, Troy. *American Hauntings*. www.prairieghosts.com.

"Tsali: Cultural Background." *The Moonlit Road*. www.themoonlitroad.com/tsali/tsali_cbg001.asp.

"Tsali in Legend." *North Carolina Museum of History*. ncmuseumofhistory.org/workshops/legends/Tslegends.html.

Unsolved Mysteries. www.unsolvedmysteries.com.

Young, Claiborne. *Cruising Guide to Coastal North Carolina: Bath* (excerpts). www.pamlico.com/bath/CGNC .

Acknowledgments

THE CREATION OF A BOOK IS FAR FROM A SOLITARY ACT. IT REQUIRES the vision and dedication of a team of people. It requires an editor, editorial assistant, artist, and staff at the publishing house to bring it alive. I feel blessed because I have the opportunity to work with a wonderful editor, Kyle Weaver, who captures my vision and guides my books along. I want to acknowledge his hard work, professionalism, and faith in me. I thank his editorial assistant, Brett Keener, who moved this book through production and labored hard to smooth out the stories within these pages. I also thank Heather Adel Wiggins, whose artwork gives the book visual life.

I want to thank my friends at the Ghost Research Foundation, who have traveled far at my request and always amaze me with their faith and love. A special thank you goes to Raymond Beck, who gave me more than just a chance to visit an amazing building; he gave me his friendship. His love for North Carolina is obvious and has infected me in a similar way. Mark and Carol Nesbitt are the dearest of friends and have been my sounding board many times. I thank them for their faith in me, their patience, and their love. I pray that one day I'll be able to repay them for their many kindnesses. Scott Crownover has been my friend and critic on occasion. I thank him for caring enough about my book to tell me the truth—even when it was not pleasant.

As always, I thank my children, who have the patience of Job. The late nights of my clicking keyboards, piling of books all around, and wrestling for the computer are over—for a brief time. But they will be the first to proudly announce that I have a new book coming soon. They are used to me and love me no matter how many times I tell them, "I can't do that, I have to write tonight." I love you, boys.

About the Author

PATTY A. WILSON LIVES IN CENTRAL PENNSYLVANIA AND WRITES ABOUT the paranormal and folklore. She is the author of *Haunted West Virginia* and the coauthor with Mark Nesbitt of *Haunted Pennsylvania* and *The Big Book of Pennsylvania Ghost Stories.* Her articles have appeared in several publications, including *FATE Magazine* and *Countyside.* Patty was cofounder of the Ghost Research Foundation, which was the first field research group to teach at the Rhine Research Center in Durham, North Carolina.